AROUND THE BOREE LOG
AND OTHER VERSES

AROUND THE BOREE LOG

AND OTHER VERSES

By

"JOHN O'BRIEN"

ANGUS AND ROBERTSON
SYDNEY · LONDON

Twenty-eighth edition, completing
82,250 copies.

Available Overseas—
ANGUS & ROBERTSON LTD.
48 Bloomsbury Street, London, W.C.1.

SET UP, PRINTED AND BOUND IN AUSTRALIA BY
HALSTEAD PRESS PTY LTD, NICKSON STREET, SYDNEY
1953

Registered in Australia for transmission by post as a book

CONTENTS

CONTENTS

CONTENTS

CONTENTS

AROUND THE BOREE LOG

Oh, stick me in the old caboose this night of wind
    and rain,
And let the doves of fancy loose to bill and coo
    again.
I want to feel the pulse of love that warmed the
    blood like wine;
I want to see the smile above this kind old land
    of mine.

So come you by your parted ways that wind the
    wide world through,
And make a ring around the blaze the way we
    used to do;
The "fountain" on the sooted crane will sing the
    old, old song
Of common joys in homely vein forgotten, ah,
    too long.

*The years have turned the rusted key, and time is
    on the jog,*
*Yet spend another night with me around the boree
    log.** *

---

* Boree (sometimes accented on the last syllable) is the
aboriginal name for the Weeping Myall—the best firewood
in Australia except Gidgee.

Now someone driving through the rain will happen
    in, I bet;
So fill the fountain up again, and leave the table
    set.
For this was ours with pride to say—and all the
    world defy—
No stranger ever turned away, no neighbour
    passed us by.

Bedad, he'll have to stay the night; the rain is going
    to pour—
So make the rattling windows tight, and close the
    kitchen door,
And bring the old lopsided chair, the tattered
    cushion, too—
We'll make the stranger happy there, the way we
    used to do.
The years have turned the rusted key, and time is
    on the jog,
Yet spend another night with me around the boree
    log.

He'll fill his pipe, and good and well, and all aglow
    within
We'll hear the news he has to tell, the yarns he has
    to spin;
Yarns—yes, and super-yarns, forsooth, to set the
    eyes agog,
And freeze the blood of trusting youth around the
    boree log.

Then stir it up and make it burn; the poker's next
    to you;
Come, let us poke it all in turn, the way we used
    to do.
There's many a memory bright and fair will tingle
    at a name—
But leave unstirred the embers there we cannot fan
    to flame.

For years have turned the rusted key, and time is
    on the jog;
Still, spend this fleeting night with me around the
    boree log.

CALLING TO ME

Through the hush of my heart in the spell of its
    dreaming
      Comes the song of a bush boy glad-hearted and
        free;
Oh, the gullies are green where the sunlight is
    streaming,
      And the voice of that youngster is calling to
      me.

It is calling to me with a haunting insistence,
      And my feet wander off on a hoof-beaten track,
Till I hear the old magpies away in the distance
      With a song of the morning that's calling me
      back.

It is calling me back, for the dew's on the clover,
      And the colours are mellow on mountain and
      tree;
Oh, the gold has gone gray in the heart of the
    rover,
      And the bush in the sunshine is calling to me.

It is calling to me, though the breezes are telling
   Gay troubadour tales to the stars as they roam;
For the tapers are lit in the humble old dwelling,
   And the love that it sheltered is calling me
     home.

It is calling me home—but the white road lies
     gleaming,
   And afar from it all must I tarry and dree;
Just an echo far off, in the hush of my dreaming,
   Is the voice of a youngster that's calling to me.

THE LITTLE IRISH MOTHER

Have you seen the tidy cottage in the straggling,
      dusty street,
  Where the roses swing their censers by the
      door?
Have you heard the happy prattle and the tramp
      of tiny feet
  As the sturdy youngsters romp around the
      floor?
Did you wonder why the wiree* comes to sing his
      sweetest song?
  Did the subtle charm of home upon you fall?
Did you puzzle why it haunted you the while you
      passed along?—
  There's a Little Irish Mother there; that's all.

When you watched the children toiling at their
      lessons in the school,
  Did you pick a winsome girleen from the rest,
With her wealth of curl a-cluster as she smiled
      upon the stool,
  In a simple Monday-morning neatness dressed?

---

* Also known as the Chocolate Wiree (pronounced "wiry"):
a very fine songster, called by ornithologists "Rufous-
breasted Whistler."

Did you mark the manly bearing of a healthy-
    hearted boy
  As he stood erect his well-conned task to tell?
Did you revel in the freshness with a pulse of
    wholesome joy?—
  There a Little Irish Mother there as well.

There's a Little Irish Mother that a lonely vigil
    keeps
  In the settler's hut where seldom stranger
    comes,
Watching by the home-made cradle where one
    more Australian sleeps
  While the breezes whisper weird things to the
    gums,
Where the settlers battle gamely, beaten down to
    rise again,
  And the brave bush wives the toil and silence
    share,
Where the nation is a-building in the hearts of
    splendid men—
  There's a Little Irish Mother always there.

There's a Little Irish Mother—and her head is
    bowed and gray,
  And she's lonesome when the evening shadows
    fall;
Near the fire she "do be thinkin'," all the "childer"
    are away,
  And their silent pictures watch her from the
    wall.

For the world has claimed them from her; they
        are men and women now,
  In their thinning hair the tell-tale silver
        gleams;
But she runs her fingers, dozing, o'er a tousled
        baby brow—
  It is "little Con" or "Bridgie" in her dreams.

There's a Little Irish Mother sleeping softly now
        at last
  Where the tangled grass is creeping all around;
And the shades of unsung heroes troop about her
        from the past
  While the moonlight scatters diamonds on the
        mound.
And a good Australian's toiling in the world of
        busy men
  Where the strife and sordid grinding cramp and
        kill;
But his eyes are sometimes misted, and his heart
        grows brave again—
  She's the Little Irish Mother to him still.

When at last the books are balanced in the settling-
        up to be,
  And our idols on the rubbish-heap are hurled,
Then the Judge shall call to honour—not the
        "stars," it seems to me,
  Who have posed behind the footlights of the
        world;

But the king shall doff his purple, and the queen
    lay by her crown,
  And the great ones of the earth shall stand aside
While a Little Irish Mother in her tattered, faded
    gown
  Shall receive the crown too long to her denied.

ONE BY ONE

With trust in God and her good man
    She settled neath the spur;
The old slab dwelling, spick and span,
    Was world enough for her;
The lamp-light kissed her raven hair
    As, when her work was done,
She lined us up beside her chair
    And taught us one by one.

And weaving memories, haunting sweet,
    With threads of weal and woe,
The years went by on velvet feet—
    We did not hear them go.
The world was calling everywhere
    Beneath the golden sun;
When silver streaked her raven hair,
    We left her one by one.

Then, turning back on cogs of pain,
    The spool that ran so fast
Unwound before her eyes again
    The pictures of the past.

The shadows played around her chair,
  Where fancy's web was spun;
When time had bleached her raven hair,
  She called us one by one.

Oh, say not that we loved her less!
  But write them to our shame,
The silence and the loneliness;
  And then the summons came—
We found the dark clouds banking there
  To hide the setting sun.
Ah, white threads in her children's hair!—
  We gathered one by one.

How quaintly sere, how small and strange
  The old home and the spur;
But stranger this—the only change
  Was wrought in us and her.
The lamp-light kissed her faded chair,
  Where, ere the sands had run,
The sheen still on her raven hair,
  She'd nursed us one by one.

Oh, vain the word that each could tell
  With full heart brimming o'er,
That we, who ever loved her well,
  Might still have loved her more!
Then back into the world of care—
  To bless till life is done—
A memory crowned with milk-white hair
  We carried one by one.

TEN LITTLE STEPS AND STAIRS

There were ten little Steps and Stairs.
  Round through the old bush home all day
  Romping about in the old bush way.
They were ten little wild March hares,
  Storming the kitchen in hungry lines,
  With their naked feet, doing mud designs,
  "All over the place like punkin vines."
There were ten little Steps and Stairs.

There were ten little Steps and Stairs.
  In their home-made frocks and their Sunday
    suits,
  Up through the church with their squeaky
    boots,
While the folk went astray in their prayers,
  They hustled along, all dressed and neat—
  Oh, they bustled a bit as they filled the seat;
  From the first to the last, the lot complete,
There were ten little Steps and Stairs.

There were ten little Steps and Stairs.
 But the years have shuffled them all about,
 Have worn them thin, and straightened them
  out
With the tramp of a hundred cares;
 Ay, and each grim scar has a tale to tell
 Of a knock and a blow and a hand that fell,
 And a break in the line, and a gap. Ah, well—
There *were* ten little Steps and Stairs.

THE TRIMMIN'S ON THE ROSARY

Ah, the memories that find me now my hair is
    turning gray,
Drifting in like painted butterflies from paddocks
    far away;
Dripping dainty wings in fancy—and the pictures,
    fading fast,
Stand again in rose and purple in the album of
    the past.
There's the old slab dwelling dreaming by the
    wistful, watchful trees,
Where the coolabahs are listening to the stories of
    the breeze;
There's a homely welcome beaming from its big,
    bright friendly eyes,
With The Sugarloaf behind it blackened in against
    the skies;
There's the same dear happy circle round the
    boree's cheery blaze
With a little Irish mother telling tales of other
    days.
She had one sweet, holy custom which I never can
    forget,
And a gentle benediction crowns her memory for
    it yet;

I can see that little mother still and hear her as she
    pleads,
"Now it's getting on to bed-time; all you childer
    get your beads."
There were no steel-bound conventions in that old
    slab dwelling free;
Only this—each night she lined us up to say the
    Rosary;
E'en the stranger there, who stayed the night upon
    his journey, knew
He must join the little circle, ay, and take his
    decade too.
I believe she darkly plotted, when a sinner hove in
    sight
Who was known to say no prayer at all, to make
    him stay the night.
Then we'd softly gather round her, and we'd
    speak in accents low,
And pray like Sainted Dominic so many years
    ago;
And the little Irish mother's face was radiant, for
    she knew
That "where two or three are gathered" He is
    gathered with them too.
O'er the paters and the aves how her reverent
    head would bend!
How she'd kiss the cross devoutly when she
    counted to the end!

And the visitor would rise at once, and brush his
    knees—and then
He'd look very, very foolish as he took the boards
    again.
She had other prayers to keep him. They were
    long, long prayers in truth;
And we used to call them "Trimmin's" in my dis-
    respectful youth.
She would pray for kith and kin, and all the friends
    she'd ever known,
Yes, and everyone of us could boast a "trimmin'"
    all his own.
She would pray for all our little needs, and every
    shade of care
That might darken o'er The Sugarloaf, she'd meet
    it with a prayer.
She would pray for this one's "sore complaint," or
    that one's "hurted hand,"
Or that someone else might make a deal and get
    "that bit of land";
Or that Dad might sell the cattle well, and seasons
    good might rule,
So that little John, the weakly one, might go away
    to school.
There were trimmin's, too, that came and went;
    but ne'er she closed without
Adding one for something special "none of you
    must speak about."

Gentle was that little mother, and her wit would
  sparkle free,
But she'd murder him who looked around while
  at the Rosary:
And if perchance you lost your beads, disaster
  waited you,
For the only one she'd pardon was "himself"—
  because she knew
He was hopeless, and 'twas sinful what excuses he'd
  invent,
So she let him have his fingers, and he cracked
  them as he went,
And, bedad, he wasn't certain if he'd counted five
  or ten,
Yet he'd face the crisis bravely, and would start
  around again;
But she tallied all the decades, and she'd block him
  on the spot,
With a "Glory, Daddah, Glory!" and he'd
  "Glory" like a shot.
She would portion out the decades to the company
  at large;
But when she reached the trimmin's she would put
  herself in charge;
And it oft was cause for wonder how she never
  once forgot,
But could keep them in their order till she went
  right through the lot.

For that little Irish mother's prayers embraced the
    country wide;
If a neighbour met with trouble, or was taken ill,
    or died,
We could count upon a trimmin'—till, in fact, it
    got that way
That the Rosary was but trimmin's to the trimmin's
    we would say.
Then "himself" would start keownrawning*—for
    the public good, we thought—
"Sure you'll have us here till mornin'. Yerra, cut
    them trimmin's short!"
But she'd take him very gently, till he softened by
    degrees—
"Well, then, let us get it over. Come now, all hands
    to their knees."
So the little Irish mother kept her trimmin's to the
    last,
Ever growing as the shadows o'er the old selection
    passed;
And she lit our drab existence with her simple
    faith and love,
And I know the angels lingered near to bear her
    prayers above,
For her children trod the path she trod, nor did
    they later spurn
To impress her wholesome maxims on their children
    in their turn.

---

* Grumbling, "grousing."

Ay, and every "sore complaint" came right, and
    every "hurted hand";
And we made a deal from time to time, and got
    "that bit of land";
And Dad did sell the cattle well; and little John,
    her pride,
Was he who said the Mass in black the morning
    that she died;
So her gentle spirit triumphed—for 'twas this,
    without a doubt,
Was the very special trimmin' that she kept so dark
    about.

    .   .   .   .   .

But the years have crowded past us, and the
    fledglings all have flown,
And the nest beneath The Sugarloaf no longer is
    their own;
For a hand has written "*finis*" and the book is
    closed for good—
There's a stately red-tiled mansion where the old
    slab dwelling stood;
There the stranger has her "evenings," and the
    formal supper's spread,
But I wonder has she "trimmin's" now, or is the
    Rosary said?
Ah, those little Irish mothers passing from us one
    by one!
Who will write the noble story of the good that
    they have done?

All their children may be scattered, and their
    fortunes windwards hurled,
But the Trimmin's on the Rosary will bless them
    round the world.

THE BIRDS WILL SING AGAIN

She saw The Helper standing near
    When grief and care oppressed;
"A Great, Big God," Who wiped the tear,
    And soothed the aching breast.
So, in the stress of sorrows piled,
    The gloom was lifted when
She pointed up and sweetly smiled
"A Great, Big God; be brave, my child,
    The birds will sing again."

When dark misfortune, hovering o'er,
    Brought woes on every hand;
And care was camping by the door,
    And drought was on the land;
When lingering hope in rags was clad,
    Her faith shone brightest then—
"A Great, Big God; so cheer up, Dad.
Don't mope about and take it bad,
    The birds will sing again."

And always some soft silver ray
    Athwart the gloom would burst
To chase the heavy clouds away,
    When things were at their worst.

Her "Great, Big God" would justify
   The trembling trust of men;
For, when the cheerless night passed by,
The sun would wink his golden eye,
   And birds would sing again.

THE OLD BUSH SCHOOL

'Tis a queer, old battered landmark that belongs to
    other years;
With the dog-leg fence around it, and its hat about
    its ears,
And the cow-bell in the gum-tree, and the bucket
    on the stool,
There's a motley host of memories round that old
    bush school—

With its seedy desks and benches, where at least
    I left a name
Carved in agricultural letters—'twas my only bid
    for fame;
And the spider-haunted ceilings, and the rafters,
    firmly set,
Lined with darts of nibs and paper (doubtless
    sticking in them yet),
And the greasy slates and blackboards, where I oft
    was proved a fool
And a blur upon the scutcheon of the old bush
    school.

There I see the boots in order—" 'lastic-sides" we
    used to wear—
With a pair of "everlastin's" cracked and dusty
    here and there;
And we marched with great "high action"—hands
    behind and eyes before—
While we murdered "Swanee River" as we
    tramped around the floor.

Still the scholars pass before me with their freckled
    features grave,
And a nickname fitting better than the name their
    mothers gave;
Tousled hair and vacant faces, and their garments
    every one
Shabby heirlooms in the family, handed down from
    sire to son.
Ay, and mine were patched in places, and half-
    masted, as a rule—
They were fashionable trousers at the old bush
    school.

There I trudged it from the Three-mile, like a
    patient, toiling brute,
With a stocking round my ankle, and my heart
    within my boot,
Morgan, Nell and Michael Joseph, Jim and Mary,
    Kate and Mart
Tramping down the sheep-track with me, little
    rebels at the heart;

Shivery grasses round about us nodding bonnets in
    the breeze,
Happy Jacks and Twelve Apostles* hurdle-racing
    up the trees,
Peewees calling from the gullies, living wonders in
    the pool—
Hard bare seats and drab gray humdrum at the old
    bush school.

Early rising in the half-light, when the morn came,
    bleak and chill;
For the little mother roused us ere the sun had
    topped the hill,
"Up, you children, late 'tis gettin'." Shook the
    house beneath her knock,
And she wasn't always truthful, and she tampered
    with the clock.

Keen she was about "the learnin'," and she told us
    o'er and o'er
Of our luck to have "the schoolin' " right against
    our very door.
And the lectures—Oh, those lectures to our stony
    hearts addressed!
"Don't be mixin' with the Regans and the Ryans
    and the rest"—

---

* These names are often applied to the same bird; but
Happy Jacks (*alias* Gray-crowned Babblers) are brown with
white markings; Twelve Apostles (*alias* Apostle-Birds) are
gray with brown wings. Peewees, in the next line, are of
course Magpie Larks.

C

"Don't be pickin' up with Carey's little talkative
    kanats"—*
Well, she had us almost thinking we were born
    aristocrats.
But we found our level early—in disaster, as a
    rule—
For they knocked "the notions" sideways at the
    old bush school.

Down the road came Laughing Mary, and the beast
    that she bestrode
Was Maloney's sorry piebald she had found beside
    the road;
Straight we scrambled up behind her, and as many
    as could fit
Clung like circus riders bare-back without bridle-
    rein or bit,
On that corrugated backbone in a merry row we
    sat—
We propelled him with our school-bags; Mary
    steered him with her hat—
And we rolled the road behind us like a ribbon
    from the spool,
"Making butter," so we called it, to the old bush
    school.

What a girl was Mary Casey in the days of long
    ago!
She was queen among the scholars, or at least we
    thought her so;

---

* The essential kanat (possibly a corruption of gnat) is
undersized, mischievous, useless and perky.

She was first in every mischief and, when over-
    whelmed by fate,
She could make delightful drawings of the teacher
    on her slate.
There was rhythm in every movement, as she gaily
    passed along
With a rippling laugh that lilted like the music of
    a song;
So we called her "Laughing Mary," and a fitful
    fancy blessed
E'en the bashful little daisies that her dainty feet
    caressed.

She had cheeks like native roses in the fullness of
    their bloom,
And she used to sing the sweetest as we marched
    around the room;
In her eyes there lurked the magic, maiden freshness
    of the morn,
In her hair the haunting colour I had seen upon the
    corn;
Round her danced the happy sunshine when she
    smiled upon the stool—
And I used to swap her dinners at the old bush
    school.

Hard the cobbled road of knowledge to the feet
    of him who plods
After fragile fragments fallen from the workshop
    of the gods;

Long the quest, and ever thieving pass the pedlars
o'er the hill
With the treasures in their bundles, but to leave us
questing still.
Mystic fires horizons redden, but each crimson
flash in turn
Only lights the empty places in the bracken and
the fern;
So in after years I've proved it, spite of pedant,
crank, and fool,
Very much the way I found it at the old bush
school.

SIX BROWN BOXER HATS

The hawker with his tilted cart pulled up beside
    the fence,
And opened out his wondrous mart with startling
    eloquence;
All sorts of toys for girls and boys upon the grass
    he spread,
And dolls, dirt-cheap, that went to sleep when
    stood upon their head;
But our male hearts were beating high for balls and
    cricket-bats
When mother, with the business eye, bought six
    brown boxer hats.

Six out-of-date extinguishers that fitted us too
    soon—
Six ugly, upturned canisters—but through the
    afternoon
Our rage and scorn were overborne to see swift
    fingers flit
With pad and trim, around the rim, to make the
    stove-pipes fit.
So Monday morning came, and six "ungrateful
    young kanats"
Went off to school like lunatics in six brown boxer
    hats.

Then friends at every meeting showed an interest
   all too rare
Or chilled our faltered greetings with the silence
   of a stare;
And comrades who, we thought, were true in-
   dulged in vulgar jeers,
While willing fists of humorists slambanged them
   round our ears;
But worst of all the social smart from taunting
   plutocrats—
"Yez pinched them from the hawker's cart, them
   six brown boxer hats."

(Dress how we will, we feel it still, when friends
   will stop to chat,
To see a broad good-humoured smile is trained
   upon the hat.)
We could not fight with wonted might, for bitter
   black distress
Was in our souls, and on our polls the hateful
   ugliness.
We faced a fine barrage of sticks; and six "broke-
   up" kanats
Went home to meet the storm in six brown battered
   boxer hats.

THE LIBEL

"The flowers have no scent, and the birds have no
      song,"
  We read in the lesson before us,
While carols enchanted came floating along,
  And lifted our hearts in the chorus.

"The landscape is sombre, and dreary, and gray,
  No colour its mantle adorning";
O'er carpets spread far in a golden array
  We tramped it to school in the morning.

"The flowers have no scent," but the wattle we
      brought
  From hill-sides and glens where we found it
Was filling the room with its glory, we thought,
  And wafting its sweetness around it.

And fragrant the greeting the eucalypts threw
  From branches of amber and sorrel;
While hard by the door a pittosporum grew—
  We called it "The Japanese Laurel."

"The birds have no song," so they told us at
　　　school;
　　But sweet in our souls was the ringing
Of notes soft and clear from the edge of the
　　　pool,
　　Where dainty gay thrushes were singing.

The magpie, the spink,* and the pretty blue
　　　wren,
　　The butcher-bird up in his eyrie,
The trills! Oh, I wish I could hear you again,
　　My dear little Chocolate Wiree!

To the ears of a stranger our birds may lack
　　　song,
　　Our flowers have no scent for the alien;
But we, who have rambled the gullies along
　　Bedecked in soft colours Australian,

We laugh them to scorn as we read the old
　　　phrase—
　　We've laughed, since, at many another—
And bless in our hearts in a chorus of praise
　　The face of our happy young mother.

---

* No apology is needed for using this name to replace
White-shouldered Caterpillar-eater.

WHEN THE CIRCUS CAME TO TOWN

When the circus came to town
With its coaches and four, and its steeds galore,
   And a band and a painted clown,
Out to the road with a shout we'd fly
To gape at the elephants trudging by,
And our hearts beat fast and our hopes ran high,
   As we followed it up and down;
For nought in the air, the sea, or sky
Could fill a spot in our youthful eye,
   When the circus came to town.

So after the show we went,
And we got in the way of the men when they
   Were rigging the circus tent,
And we knew that we stood on holy ground,
As we followed an empty van around—
And got for ourselves a belting sound,
   Which a charm to the business lent.
But we wagged it from school behind the pound,
Till some Jack Pudding our shelter found
   And word to headquarters sent.

When the circus came to town,
We swallowed hot tea with tears of glee,
   And rushed in a tumult down;
We took quite the full of our shilling's worth,
And roared at the dummy's ponderous girth,
Or yelled in a salvo of noisy mirth
   At the tricks of the painted clown.
Oh, wondrous thoughts in our minds had birth,
And we felt that the band was the best on earth,
   When the circus came to town.

We fondly recalled the scene,
Horses that pranced, and eyes entranced,
   And the smell of the kerosene;
The mule, and the monkey, and tall giraffe,
The "juggerlin'-man" with his magic staff,   .
The girl who went round with her photograph
   (And oh, but we thought her a queen!)
We started a show on our own behalf,
"Performed" on the back of a poddy calf,
   And sighed for the might-have-been.

Now the circus comes to town,
And it rattles along, and a bare-foot throng
   Is pacing it up and down;
And the elephants trudge as they trudged of
     yore,
With the shabby shebangs, and the steeds
     galore;

But the glee of the youngsters who shout and
    roar
  At the tricks of the painted clown
Is balm to my soul, and I call *encore*
To the frowsy old jokes I've heard before,
  When the circus came to town.

HIS FATHER

We meet him first in frills immersed,
By everyone caressed and nursed,
  A bonny baby—rather!
But, though they please his every whim,
Fill up his comforts to the brim,
And "ketchie ketchie" say to him,
  He whimpers for his father;
Nor any plan of all the clan,
Nor fiction *re* the bogie-man
  Can coax him from his father.

Then, done with frocks and curly locks,
Promoted into knickerbocks,
  This wholesome, healthy laddie
Will entertain the other kid
With tales of what his Daddy did;
He lives a splendid dream amid
  Heroic deeds of Daddy.
In grief or mirth he's proved his worth;
The greatest man in all this earth
  Is Knickerbocker's Daddy.

Long pants at last, and stretching fast—
Said pants are what is termed "half-mast,"
    And most attenuated—
Great notions now his head doth hold,
And schemes of mischief manifold,
He talks as though he had a cold
    In slang adulterated.
He has the shy and shifty eye,
He burns tobacco on the sly,
    In black butts immolated.

Now mark his ways these latter days;
He sounds no more his father's praise
    With fervent admiration;
In fact, his father's got to be
An out-of-date necessity,
A clog upon his destiny
    And youthful recreation.
As like as not, in anger hot,
He'll speak of him as "my old pot"—
    A homely appellation.

Another page, the dandy stage
That starts at eighteen years of age.
    His talk is all of horses;
He now selects his socks and ties
To match the colour of his eyes;
He's learnt the art of looking wise,
    And on his Dad's resources
He gaily goes in Yankee clothes,
And backs the ponies through his nose
    At most suburban courses.

He swaggers when amongst the men,
And takes a "tonic" now and then
   To make a good impression;
And by the hour he will relate
The deeds that made him truly great,
Just pausing to expectorate
   By way of a digression.
And here, mayhap, to fill a gap
He'll just allude to his "old chap"—
   A valueless possession.

Next, older grown, the rolling-stone
Is out in business on his own.
   We find him somewhat later
With this new burden to his song,
"Your old contraptions all are wrong."
He's going to move the world along,
   His fortune's own dictator.
And, all the while, he can but smile
About the antiquated style
   That ruled the poor old Pater.

We meet him next somewhat perplexed,
By business problems badly vexed—
   The other fellow's caught him.
Then, while he's chafing in the thrall,
Dad in some ways, he can recall,
Was not so hopeless after all
   As in the past he thought him;

At any rate, he's free to state
The old man's head was "screwed on
    straight,"
  And knocking round had taught him.

We come again to find him when
He's stood within the lion's den,
  And trembled at disaster.
It was the Dad who pulled him through,
And now he will admit to you
The old man knows a thing or two;
  Then, troubles coming faster,
He's very glad to mount his prad
And go and have a word with Dad,
  For Dad is now the Master.

But further on, life's springtime gone,
The winter snow his brows upon,
  Adown the current carried,
He'll show you with a tender glance
A photo framed with elegance—
The old man in the "bell-bot" pants,
  The suit in which he tarried
That day in town a joy to crown
(Most likely 'twas a "reach-me-down"),
  The day the Dad was married.

His dreams dispersed, the bubble burst,
We find him where we found him first,
  Right proud about his father;

And now again he writes in sooth
The head-line of his early youth,
But he observes—unwelcome truth,
    At times he's worried, rather—
His hopeful son has just begun
The same old devious course to run:
    And now it's he's the father.

THE KOOKABURRAS

Fall the shadows on the gullies, fades the purple
    from the mountain;
And the day that's passing outwards down the
    stairways of the sky,
With its kindly deeds and sordid on its folded page
    recorded,
Waves a friendly hand across the range to bid the
    world "good-bye."
Comes a buoyant peal of laughter from the tall,
    white, slender timber,
Rugged mirth that floods the bushland with the
    joy of brotherhood,
With the rustic notes sonorous of a happy laughing
    chorus,
When the kookaburras bless the world because the
    world is good.

Oh, 'tis good and clean and wholesome when we
    take the sheep-track homewards,
And the kindly kitchen chimney flaps its homely
    bannerets;

D

All our twigs of effort, shooting golden promise
    for the fruiting,
Bring a night in peace enfolded that a useful day
    begets.
Hopeful dreams, their visions weaving, steel our
    hearts against to-morrow,
And we dare the challenge, strengthened by to-
    day's assaults withstood;
Beam the pregnant days before us; and another
    laughing chorus
Wraps the world in rippling revelry, because the
    world is good.

Loving eyes to watch our coming, loving arms to
    twine around us—
Tender tendrils, soft and silken, firmer far than
    iron stay—
All our little world upholding, gentle hearts and
    home enfolding,
And a cheery, friendly neighbour dropping in
    upon his way:
Mellow joy the soul refreshes with the scented
    breath of heaven,
With the whispered songs of other spheres, here-
    after understood:
Angels keep their sure watch o'er us: and another
    laughing chorus
Flings a vesper blessing round the world, because
    the world is good.

PETER NELSON'S FIDDLE

Do you ever dream you hear it, you who went the
    lonely track?
  Do you ever hear its simple melodies
Tossing round deserted beaches, with the flotsam
    and the wrack,
  When the moonlight sprinkles silver on the
    trees?

Do you hearken now, I wonder, when the birds
    have gone to rest,
  And the blotted book of day once more is shut?
When the saffron stains have faded, and the swans
    have vanished west,
  Does your heart remember Peter Nelson's hut?

Lonely, stooped old Peter Nelson, with his "most
    peculiar" ways,
  With the clean-cut face, and hair as white as
    snow!
Something lingering round the old man seemed to
    tell of better days,
  Seemed to hint of love and laughter long ago.

Kindly silence wrapped the bushland; every war-
ring note was still;
   Soft heart-tremors stirred, and smiling eyes grew
dim.
Weaving fancies went the fiddle; dreams prophetic
made us thrill—
   From the grave the visions stretched their hands
to him.

There was rapture in the stillness; there were voices
in the night;
   Trooped the angels with a beat of velvet
wings;
And the stars stood still and listened, and the
moon's face, strangely white,
   Kissed the sleeping world to dreams of better
things.

Joy was lit in every corner, love was smiling at
our side,
   Golden glamour o'er the dawning days was
cast;
Gaily, gaily sang the fiddle, while we marched with
swinging stride
   Through the flowers that hid the failures of the
past.

Do you ever dream you hear it? Does it bring the
vision back,
   With the curlew, and the moonlight on the
trees?

Do the wavelets ripple shoreward with the flotsam
    as the wrack,
  When a fiddle plays the simple melodies?

Lonely, bent old Peter Nelson with the quaint,
    uncommon ways,
  "Spruced and tidied" when the book of day was
    shut,
With the dim light in the window, and the friends
    of better days
  Summoned round him by the fiddle in the hut.

THE CHURCH UPON THE HILL

A simple thing of knotted pine
    And corrugated tin;
But still, to those who read, a sign,
A fortress on the farthest line
    Against the march of sin.

Though rich man's gold was lacking quite,
    We built it strong and sure,
With willing hands and (Faith's delight)
The savings spared, the widow's mite,
    The shillings of the poor.

Nor could it fail to meet the eye
    And reverent thoughts instil,
As there above the township high,
And pointing always to the sky,
    It stood upon the hill.

And through our lives in wondrous ways
    Its holy purpose led
From limpid lisping cradle-days
To where the silent moonlight lays
    White hands upon the dead.

For when the Holy Morning strung
  Its beads upon the grass,
You'd see us driving—old and young—
The tall white graceful trees among,
  On every road to Mass.

It brought the brave young mother there,
  Surrounded by her brood,
To wrap their tiny hearts in prayer,
And teach them how to cast their care
  Upon the Holy Rood.

It watched the little bush girl grow,
  And kept her life from harm,
Till, spotless as the virgin snow
In wreath and veil, it saw her go
  Upon her husband's arm.

It blessed strong, trembling shoulders bent:
  Helped many a soul in thrall
To climb again the steep ascent,
And reft the grim entanglement
  That brought about the fall.

It soothed the gray old mother's pain,
  A-swaying while she told
Her rosary o'er and o'er again,
For griefs that rent her heart in twain—
  So new, and ah, so old!

(There's "that poor boy who went astray,"
   And lined her gentle brow;
There's "them that's wand'rin' fur away,"
And "them that's in their grave to-day"
   And "beck'nin' " to her now.)

Refuge it gave the weary heart,
   Beyond the sordid din
And conflict of the crowded mart,
One sweet, sequestered nook apart,
   Where all might enter in.

Though high and grand cathedrals shine,
   To my mind grander still
Is that wee church of knotted pine,
That rampart on the outer line
   That stood upon the hill.

CURRAJONG

Old Father Pat! They'll tell you still with mingled
    love and pride
Of stirring deeds that live and thrill the quiet
    country-side;
And when they praise his *tours-de-force*, be sure it
    won't be long
Before they talk about his horse—the old gray
    Currajong.

For twenty years he drove him through the bush
    and round the town,
Until the old white stager knew the parish upside
    down;
He'd take his time, and calculate, and have his
    wilful way,
And stop at every Catholic gate to bid them all
    good day.

But well I mind the stories told when Father Pat
    was young—
At least, when he was not so old—his scattered flock
    among;

When health and strength were on his side, you'd
    see him swing along
With that clean, easy, sweeping stride that marked
    old Currajong.

Through all the years he ne'er was late the second
    Mass to say,
And twenty miles he'd "duplicate," and pass us
    on the way.
Hard-held and beating clean tattoos, the old
    gray, stepping kind,
Like gravel from his twinkling shoes would fling
    the miles behind.

And often some too daring lad, a turn of speed
    to show,
Would straighten up his sleepy prad and give the
    priest a "go";
But, faith, he found what others found, and held
    the lesson long,
That nothing in the country round could move
    with Currajong.

And, oh, the din! and, oh, the fuss! mere words
    were vain to tell
Of how they stopped the night with us; and don't
    I mind it well?
The boree log ablaze "inside," and gay with rug
    and mat;
The "front-room," to the world denied, made
    snug for Father Pat.

We knew his distant hoof-beats; ay, and grief
    they could forebode;
So, when we heard a horse go by, clean-stepping
    down the road,
Round many a log-fire burning bright there
    passed the word along,
"There's someone sick and sore the night; I'll bet
    that's Currajong."

Whereat you'd hear the old men tell—perhaps a
    trifle add—
Of some sick-call remembered well, when "so-
    and-so took bad."
"You couldn't see your hand in front." " 'Twas
    rainin' pitchforks, too."
"The doctor jibbed, to put it blunt—but Father
    Pat went through."

Ay, he went through in shine or shade; so, when
    the days were fair,
And at our simple sports we played, 'twas good
    to see him there;
And under troubled, angry skies, when all the
    world went wrong,
With aching hearts and misted eyes we watched
    for Currajong.

We watched, and never watched in vain, what-
    ever might befall.
When summoned to the bed of pain, he answered
    to the call.

He came through rain or storm or heat; and in
    the darkest night
We heard his hoofs the music beat, we saw the
    welcome light.

And when again, with plumes ahead and horses
    stepping slow,
We followed on, behind our dead, the road all
    men must go,
A loitering line, with knots and gaps, the funeral
    passed along,
And half a mile of lurching traps was led by
    Currajong.

But, as the good priest older grew, and aches and
    troubles came,
His buggy and the white horse, too, were stricken
    much the same.
The springs went down the side he sat, and altar-
    boys and such
Kept sliding in on Father Pat, and woke him at
    the touch.

Then, pensioned off at last and done, a sorry thing
    it stood,
With sagging cobwebs round it spun, and nest-
    eggs in the hood.
Just once a year it lived again, and groaned and
    creaked along
To fetch the bishop from the train with limping
    Currajong.

Ah, newer methods, younger men! the times are
    moving fast,
And but in dreams we tread again the wheel-ruts
    of the past;
The eyes are filmed that watched of old, the
    kindly hearts are still,
And silent tombstones white and cold are glim-
    mering on the hill.

While scorching up the road, belike, with singing
    gears alive
The curate on his motor-bike hits up his forty-
    five;
But tender, tingling memories swell, and love will
    linger long
In all the stirring yarns they tell about Old
    Currajong.

THE HELPING HAND

When that hour comes when I shall sit alone,
And ponder on the things that were, but are no
    more,
The while the weird night-breeze's dirge-like
    monotone
Is sobbing fitful anthems round the door;

When homing billows moan and croon un-
    checked,
And no light glimmers on the ocean's broad
    expanse;
When all my anxious hopes are safe in port, or
    wrecked
On sharp uncharted rocks of circumstance;

When I have lived my life, and Time at last
Displays the mottled fate the sisters three have
    spun,
When the night's mystic, sombre, starless cloak is
    cast
Around the naked shoulders of the sun;

I shall be tired, I know, and long to rest,
And o'er the past sleep's veil of sweet oblivion
    draw,
To feel myself drawn softly, dream-like on the
    breast
Of life's ebb-tide that laps the Eternal Shore.

When that hour comes, and I am drifting slow
To azure distance stretching on, and on, and on;
When earth's coast-lights are dim and blurred and
    burning low,
And other stars rise other worlds upon;

I shall not fear to meet my Master's gaze,
Nor, like an idling child, His Searching Presence
    shun,
E'en though no herald trumpet-voice pronounce
    my praise,
And earth-won hero garlands wear I none.

E'en though the best the world shall know of
    me,
When mouldering clay is laid with kindred clay
    again,
Is but a stone on which the stars shine carelessly
Smooth-polished by the fingers of the rain:

I shall not fear to stand before His Face
And answer for the schemes I reared on shifting
    sand,

Whereon the waves are trailing albs of pointed
  lace,
If on my way I've lent the helping hand

To fellow-pilgrims toiling at my side,
Who, worn and weary, faint and fall beside the
  road,
If here betimes the blinding, scalding tear I've
  dried,
Or soothed a heart, or eased a galling load,

For He shall say "Your name in dust is hid,
No thought or word has earned you immortality;
Immortal only are the kindly things you did—
Amen I say, you did them unto me."

VALE, FATHER PAT

Yes, that's the hardest hand at all upon my frosted
    head—
That telegram that brought the news that Father
    Pat is dead—
I cannot grip its message yet; we were such cronies,
    that
The world is not a world to-night without poor
    Father Pat.

Nigh eighty years I've known him now. Since ever
    we were boys
Across the sea in Ireland, each other's cares and
    joys
We've shared as with their leaden step they strode
    across the mat;
The kindest heart that ever beat is stilled in Father
    Pat.

They knew him round the country wide; from
    here to Carrathool
The teamster toiling by his dray, the youngsters
    home from school,

E

Would greet him with a curt "good day," and
    shyly pull the hat
Down farther on the forehead in respect for
    Father Pat.

I see him in my mind to-night, a diamond in the
    rough,
A kindly soul that hid the gold, but showed the
    sterner stuff—
The wise old eye, the homely face, the scant hairs
    pasted flat
Across the wide wise baldness of the head of Father
    Pat;

The collar caught with honest tape when fleeting
    studs had gone;
The suit that said good-bye to cut the day he put
    it on;
The handsome stock the sisters built, the tassels on
    the hat,
The stout umbrella in the hand of manly Father
    Pat.

I see the ordered sitting-room he'll never enter
    more,
The ivory bead-crowned crucifix, the font behind
    the door,
The parish books, the registers and, handy where
    he sat,
The well-thumbed breviary that warmed the heart
    of Father Pat.

A man of method all the time—the pigeon-holes
    a-line,
A dozen keys upon a chain, his pockets filled with
    twine.
His actions told the time of day, and rivalled e'en
    in that
The sober clock that ticked away the life of Father
    Pat.

He used to run the curate on the lines he ran
    himself;
A list of parish duties stood upon the mantel-
    shelf,
As binding as the decalogue, so all-embracing
    that
The bishop had to keep the step, when guest of
    Father Pat.

He'd argue till the cows came home, and never
    know a doubt;
But when he "showed the p'liteness," it was then,
    my boy, look out!
He'd lay the shoneen* by the heels, and shake him
    like a rat;
He wasn't worth a straw, bedad, when trimmed by
    Father Pat.

His sermons were tremendous things, and thunder-
    bolts would drop;
The trouble with poor Father Pat was when and
    how to stop.

---

* An over-smart would-be gentleman; a term of contempt.

Theology? don't mention it! he'd talk the bishop
    flat;
One half was Father Gury, and the rest was Father
    Pat.

I'd quoted him so often to the young lads round
    about
To show that we old fellows still were far from
    petered out,
Could take a hand at ceremonies, could sing a Mass
    and that;
So when we had a big day here I called on Father
    Pat.

He came—but didn't conquer, faith, though every
    nerve was strained;
He'd waved his hand to rubrics on the day he was
    ordained;
He went along his old, old way in broken notes
    and flat—
To tell the truth, I felt ashamed for once of Father
    Pat.

These young lads build their castles up, and fancy's
    beacons glow.
Ah well, poor Father Pat and I went through that
    years ago;
And some of those ideals are dead, and some we've
    jested at,
And some are where the failures wait for me and
    Father Pat.

Though brighter far the morning seems than does
    the setting sun,
Still, they but carry on the work by such as us
    begun.
We blazed the tracks they tread to-day—at least
    they'll grant us that—
The men who sailed in sixty-five along with Father
    Pat.

We left the friendly stars astern, the Irish lights
    agleam,
We dared the seas in sailing-ships before the days
    of steam,
We faced a weird wild waste of world that brave
    men trembled at:
No shipside welcome met the men who came with
    Father Pat.

We turned our horses' heads out west, beyond the
    farthest track,
With nothing but an alien star to light the journey
    back.
The echoes mocked us as we went, and silence
    startled sat
When out beyond the rim of things we marched
    with Father Pat.

We said our Mass in canvas tents, and neath the
    gnarléd trees;
Of red-gum slabs and sheets of bark we built our
    sanctuaries;

Our axes rang on timbered slopes above the mining
  flat,
And church and school and convent mark the path
  of Father Pat.

We made our bow to wild and waste, and hard-
  ships worse than those;
We leave a gracious golden land that blossoms like
  the rose.
Far defter hands may now adorn the work we
  laboured at,
But granite base and buttressed wall were built by
  Father Pat.

Well may his arms drop idly down at eighty years
  of age;
His story goes behind him with no stain upon its
  page.
I'll bet he played the innings through and carried
  out his bat,
And none dare hint "retiring hurt" in front of
  Father Pat.

And with him goes the little band that sailed in
  sixty-five;
A dreamer by his lamp to-night is all that's left
  alive.
Poor Father James, and Father Ned, and jovial
  Father Mat
Are waiting out beyond the dark to welcome
  Father Pat.

I'll not attend the obsequies: I feel I could not
    face
The office that I know so well, and see his vacant
    place:
We saw a generation pass while side by side we
    sat:
Another starts its march to-day—without us,
    Father Pat.

They'll wonder why I am not there—I, last of
    all the band—
To take farewell of him that's gone; but he will
    understand.
We'll have a little requiem my own loved altar
    at,
And just ourselves—alive and dead—shall chant it,
    Father Pat.

JOSEPHINE

The presbytery has gone to pot since this house-
    keeper came;
She's up-to-date and stylish, but the place is not
    the same
Since Death's hard summons robbed me of the
    sterling old machine,
That wore out in my service here—my faithful
    Josephine.

Poor Josephine, she knew me well—and, faith,
    she ought to know;
For since the bishop sent me here, some thirty
    years ago,
My one and only manager, my right-hand man
    she'd been;
I never had a word against my trusted Josephine.

She pottered round the place herself for thirty
    years and more—
This new one has a thuckeen now to sweep and
    mind the door.

And entertain with parish chat each gossiping
   voteen*
She'd have no thuckeen near the place, would
   crabbéd Josephine.

They tell me this one's up-to-date—too up-to-
   date for me;
I tremble at her polished floors, and modern
   cookery,
The old man finds the old ways best—old springs
   were twice as green—
I've heard His Lordship praise the stews of
   clever Josephine.

My study was my sanctum once—a castle all my
   own—
But this one with her natty ways can't leave the
   place alone.
Her fingers ache to tidy up; and, when she's
   extra clean,
I sit a stranger in my room and sigh for Josephine.

She says that table's "awful" and it drives her
   to despair;
Perhaps it does, but method's in what seems
   confusion there—
I know where every paper is, each book and
   magazine.
That jumbled pile was sacred in the eyes of
   Josephine.

* A person who exaggerates his or her religious devotion.

This new one hides my things away in pigeon-
    hole and drawer,
And, faith, she does her job so well, they're lost
    for evermore.
She'll have to learn to let things be as they have
    ever been—
Just make the bed, and sweep the floor, the
    same as Josephine.

And yet no sthreel was Josephine, for quick was
    she to note
My native country's colour coming gently
    through my coat;
I teased her—said she ought to like the wearing
    of the green;
She couldn't see a joke at all, poor, solemn
    Josephine.

She used to hide my battered hats; my old biret-
    tas, too,
Just when I had them broken in, would disappear
    from view.
I wondered where my wardrobe went, until by
    chance I'd seen
A tramp in full pontificals subscribed by
    Josephine.

I mind the time the bishop came, one day in early
    spring.
We brought him round to see the school, and hear
    the children sing;

Bedad, I was a toff that day; you'd think I was
a dean,
Or some commercial traveller—my thanks to
Josephine.

My coat was pressed, just like a swell's; the
breeches that I wore
Had creases in them fore and aft like new ones
from the store.
I smelt like some old motor-car, exuding kero-
sene;
I noted, too, the furtive glance of anxious
Josephine.

She watched His Lordship's portly form pass
proudly o'er the mat,
His Majesty the curate next, with gloves and
shiny hat;
I'd stuck an old biretta on, that better days had
seen;
She came and dragged it off my head—ah, wisha,
Josephine!

It sometimes strikes me, now she's gone, she'd
no drawbacks at all:
Her features just a shade severe, her age can-
onical,
In fashions of her mother's day she trod her way
serene,
And wasteful ways of worldly dames disgusted
Josephine.

She knew the place from back to front, she knew
    the parish through,
And those who never went to Mass, and those
    who did, she knew;
The hours arranged for this and that—she had
    the whole routine—
And oftentimes to ease a doubt I went to
    Josephine.

She thought I couldn't make mistakes, not even
    if I tried;
She felt the Holy Ghost would send a mitre ere
    I died;
She lay in wait for wagging tongues—and, faith,
    her own was keen;
God help the one who dared complain in front
    of Josephine!

The people called her "curate," yes, and "bishop"
    too, I hear;
They even called her "parish-priest"—in dis-
    respect, I fear.
They told me that she'd "roon" the church—too
    long with me she'd been;
But only death could give the sack to faithful
    Josephine.

Ah, soft and sweet be sleep to her who friendless
    trod her track
Along the beaten road of life that knows no
    turning back.

I marked the splendid Irish faith that met the
    closing scene,
And heard the beat of angels' wings that came
    for Josephine.

She's in her lonely grave to-night beneath the
    Murray pines,
And haply in their breeze-swept song a requiem
    divines:
The people raised a little stone to keep her
    memory green,
And handed to the winds and rain the name of
    Josephine.

How quickly have the days gone by! she's dead—
    now, let me see—
She's dead twelve months: to-morrow is her
    anniversary:
Now who's the Saint to-morrow? Ah, a semi—
    "Hedwig, Queen."
I'll use the black—and may God rest the soul
    of Josephine!

THE OLD MASS SHANDRYDAN

I can see it in my dreaming o'er a gap of thirty
years,
And the rattle of its boxes still is music in my
ears:
With a bow to family vanity it rises from the
past
As the pride of the selection where my humble
youth was cast.
It was fashioned in a nightmare by some wander-
ing genius,
And it wasn't quite a waggon, and it wasn't quite
a 'bus;
'Twas an old four-wheeled gazabo that was
something in between,
And the wheels were painted yellow, and the rest
was painted green
(It would waken lively interest in the anti-
quarian)
And 'twas known to all the country as the Old
Mass Shandrydan.

It did duty on a week-day in a dozen ways and
    more,
And it seemed just made to order for whate'er
    'twas wanted for;
It would cart the chaff to market, carry wood
    and hay in turn,
And the neighbours in rotation used to cadge
    the old concern.
But the Sundays we were due for Mass would
    cancel every loan,
For the Little Irish Mother then would claim it
    for her own.
She inspected it the day before (and criticized
    it, too),
And the ten of us were set to work to make it
    look like new.
There was one to every yellow wheel—ay, one
    to every spoke;
One to nail a piece of hardwood on the part "them
    Careys" broke:
Another from the floor of it the chips and straw
    would rake,
While the Dad went searching rubbish-heaps for
    old boots for the brake:
So we rubbed and scrubbed and hammered up,
    and beat the rattertan
Till it stood in all its glory as the Old Mass
    Shandrydan.

When at last, with velvet sandals shod, the Holy
    Morning crept
Through the mists above The Sugarloaf, that
    silent vigil kept
O'er a little old slab dwelling which the years
    have brushed away,
You would hear the Little Mother stirring round
    before the day,
Rousing sleepy heads from blankets, washing
    faces, doing hair,
Scolding, coaxing, bustling, breathless in her
    hurry everywhere.
Half the night before she laboured, and we'd
    hear her come and go
With the Sunday suits of "reach-me-downs" to
    place them in a row.
There was this to patch, and that to darn, and
    something else to mend;
She would see to every single thing before her
    work would end,
To the dresses and the pinnies—oh, the memory
    she had!—
There were lace-up boots for Morgan, and a clean
    white shirt for Dad.
And the hubbub and the murder that the house-
    hold used to make,
When she had us tumbled out of bed, and pain-
    fully awake.
Here a voice in anguish lifted to announce a
    button gone;

Someone calling from the back-room "Mum,
    what socks will I put on?"
While "Himself" was like a Bolshevik athirst
    for human blood,
Shouting "Mother," as he wrastled with a frac-
    tious collar-stud.
But she kept the tumult under till she had us
    spick and span,
Packed like pickles in a bottle in the Old Mass
    Shandrydan.

We had ten good miles to drive to Mass—and
    Mass was sharp at eight;
But we'd never hear the end of it if something
    kept us late;
So we started ere the morning hung its bunting
    in the sky,
And the kookaburras chortled as we rumbled
    slowly by.
For the frost was on the barley, and the rime
    was on the trees,
And our little faces smarted with the whip-lash
    of the breeze,
Still we watched the branches redden to the first
    kiss of the sun
And we counted all the cart-wheels that the busy
    spiders spun,
Then the magpies sang to greet us, and our little
    hearts began
To forget that we were shivering in the Old
    Mass Shandrydan.

F

So the old contraption lumbered, safely towed,
as Dad knew how,

By a pair of hefty elephants promoted from the
plough,

And it rattled like a saw-mill, and it thundered
like a dray;

Faith, you'd hear the circus coming a half-a-
dozen miles away!

All along the road the neighbours used to take
the time from us,

For they never made a start until they heard
our omnibus;

Then a shrill soprano shouted, "Put the horses
in the van,

"Them's The Sugarloaf O'Briens in the Old Mass
Shandrydan."

We were first to Carey's Crossing, first to reach
Moloney's Mill,

But the opposition caught us as we laboured up
the hill;

Then the air became electric as they tried to pass
us by,

For "Himself" for family reasons (which I
needn't specify)

Kept the road in deadly earnest, and would never
seem to hear

The abuse of the procession that was gathering
in the rear.

Oh, they whistled and they shouted till their
    feelings overflowed,
But the old man in the Dreadnought was the
    master of the road.
It was suicide to bump it, and the horses wouldn't
    shy,
So he trundled on before them with a bad look
    in his eye.
Then, as suddenly the whistling and the banter-
    ing shouting ceased
And a solemn hush denoted the arrival of the
    priest,
Would a fine "good Catholic" thunder "Yerra,
    shame upon you, man!
Pull one side there, Pat O'Brien, with your Old
    Mass Shandrydan."

Pull! Bedad, he'd pull the town down when His
    Reverence hove in sight,
Pulled his hat off with the left hand, and pipe
    out with the right;
Pulled his family in the gutter, pulled the horses
    off their feet,
And a shower of small O'Briens went skedad-
    dling from the seat.
Then they rattled loudly past us, and a wild
    stampede began,
For they all had family reasons to outpace the
    other man.
There were buggies, traps, and turnouts there
    of every shape and rig;

There were Murphys in a spring-cart, and the
    Caseys in a gig;
There were Barnes' ponies pounding twixt a
    gallop and a trot,
While the Careys with their pacing-mare went
    sailing past the lot.
Faith, we had it in for Carey, and our disrespect
    increased
At the cheek of "them there Careys who would
    try to beat the priest."
No, we wouldn't stoop to things like that; we'd
    act the gentleman
Half a mile behind the others in the Old Mass
    Shandrydan.

It's a long way back I'm gazing, and the stage
    has changed since then;
Just an echo finds me sometimes, bringing back
    the scene again.
Oh, the heart beats slower measure than it used
    to beat, alas,
When a Little Irish Mother dressed us all in
    time for Mass.
I have lounged in fast expresses, I have travelled
    first saloon,
I have heard the haunting music that the winds
    and waters croon,
I have seen the road careering from a whirring
    motor-car,
Where the Careys couldn't pass us, or our sense
    of fitness jar;

But the world is somehow smaller, somehow less
    enchanting than
When I saw it o'er the tail-board of the Old
    Mass Shandrydan.

PITCHIN' AT THE CHURCH

On the Sunday morning mustered,
    Yarning at our ease;
Buggies, traps and jinkers clustered
    Underneath the trees,
Horses tethered to the fences;
Thus we hold our conferences
Waiting till the priest commences—
    Pitchin' at the Church.

Sheltering in the summer's shining
    Where the shadows fall;
When the winter's sun is pining,
    Lined along the wall;
Yarning, reckoning, ruminating,
"Yeos" and lambs and wool debating,
Squatting, smoking, idly waiting—
    Pitchin' at the Church.

Young bloods gathered from the others
    Tell their dreamings o'er;
Beaded-bonneted old mothers
    Grouped around the door;

Dainty bush girls, trim and fairy,
All that's neat and sweet and airy—
Nell, and Kate, and Laughing Mary—
    Pitchin' at the Church.

Up comes someone briskly driving,
    "Cutting matters fine":
All his "fam'ly lot" arriving
    Wander in a line
Off in some precise direction,
Till they find their proper section,
Greet it with an interjection—
    Pitchin' at the Church.

"Mornun', Jack." "Good mornun', Martin."
    "Keepin' pretty dry!"
"When d'you think you'll finish cartin'?"
    "Prices ain't too high?"
Round about the yarnin' strayin'—
Dances, sickness—frocks surveyin'—
Wheat is "growed," the "hens is layin'"—
    Pitchin' at the Church.

SAID HANRAHAN

"We'll all be rooned," said Hanrahan,
　　In accents most forlorn,
Outside the church, ere Mass began,
　　One frosty Sunday morn.

The congregation stood about,
　　Coat-collars to the ears,
And talked of stock, and crops, and drought,
　　As it had done for years.

"It's lookin' crook," said Daniel Croke;
　　"Bedad, it's cruke, me lad,
For never since the banks went broke
　　Has seasons been so bad."

"It's dry, all right," said young O'Neil,
　　With which astute remark
He squatted down upon his heel
　　And chewed a piece of bark.

And so around the chorus ran
　　"It's keepin' dry, no doubt."
"We'll all be rooned," said Hanrahan
　　"Before the year is out.

"The crops are done; ye'll have your work
    To save one bag of grain;
From here way out to Back-o'-Bourke
    They're singin' out for rain.

"They're singin' out for rain," he said,
    "And all the tanks are dry."
The congregation scratched its head,
    And gazed around the sky.

"There won't be grass, in any case,
    Enough to feed an ass;
There's not a blade on Casey's place
    As I came down to Mass."

"If rain don't come this month," said Dan,
    And cleared his throat to speak—
"We'll all be rooned," said Hanrahan,
    "If rain don't come this week."

A heavy silence seemed to steal
    On all at this remark;
And each man squatted on his heel,
    And chewed a piece of bark.

"We want a inch of rain, we do,"
    O'Neil observed at last;
But Croke "maintained" we wanted two
    To put the danger past.

"If we don't get three inches, man,
  Or four to break this drought,
We'll all be rooned," said Hanrahan,
  "Before the year is out."

In God's good time down came the rain;
  And all the afternoon
On iron roof and window-pane
  It drummed a homely tune.

And through the night it pattered still,
  And lightsome, gladsome elves
On dripping spout and window-sill
  Kept talking to themselves.

It pelted, pelted all day long,
  A-singing at its work,
Till every heart took up the song
  Way out to Back-o'-Bourke.

And every creek a banker ran,
  And dams filled overtop;
"We'll all be rooned," said Hanrahan,
  "If this rain doesn't stop."

And stop it did, in God's good time;
  And spring came in to fold
A mantle o'er the hills sublime
  Of green and pink and gold.

And days went by on dancing feet,
   With harvest-hopes immense,
And laughing eyes beheld the wheat
   Nid-nodding o'er the fence.

And, oh, the smiles on every face,
   As happy lad and lass
Through grass knee-deep on Casey's place
   Went riding down to Mass.

While round the church in clothes genteel
   Discoursed the men of mark,
And each man squatted on his heel,
   And chewed his piece of bark.

"There'll be bush-fires for sure, me man,
   There will, without a doubt;
We'll all be rooned," said Hanrahan,
   "Before the year is out."

THE TIDY LITTLE BODY

Faith, and little Miss McCroddie was the tidy little
    body,
    Just as trim and prim and handy as you'd ever
        wish to see
    (She was well upon the weather-beaten side of
        thirty-three);
And she'd chuckle and she'd titter when the people
    used to twit her
    On the most pronounced attentions of one Lanty
        Hallissey
    (Now this Lanty was a bachelor of some
        antiquity).

Well, he'd said good-bye to fifty; he was solemn,
    he was thrifty,
    And he'd come to Mass each Sunday decorated
        handsomely
    (With an eye upon the Tidy Little Body, don't
        you see);
And you'd see him titivated in a much abbrevi-
    ated
    Kind o' sort o' style of swallow-tail that flogged
        him viciously
    (Which it needed the judicious use of treacle at
        the knee);

And his hat was like a Quaker's; but some fifteen
  hundred acres
    More than evened up the lee-way of the said
      deficiency
    (Faith, he had a tidy cottage on the little
      property).
So, when Mass at length was over, round his jinker
  he would hover,
    While the women teased the Tidy Little Body
      merrily
    (And my hero was unconscious of their jesting,
      homely glee);

There he'd fool about, and truckle with a strap or
  with a buckle,
    And tighten this, and loosen that, a-gammon he
      do be
    (With the eye out for the Tidy Little Body,
      don't you see).
And the more they used to tease her, well, the
  more it seemed to please her;
    And she wriggled and she giggled, and she
      tittered girlishly—
    "Oh, it's all so very silly. Picture Mr. Hal-
      lissey!"

*But, bedad, for all her stricture on the paintin' of
  the picture,
    There were some of 'em a-bouncin' in the
      swithers—true for me—
    When the Tidy Little Body married Lanty
      Hallissey.*

THE PILLAR OF THE CHURCH

Faith, 'tis good to see him comin' when the bell
    for Mass is flingin'
Gladsome golden notes appealin' on the Sabbath-
    softened air,
Sweet compellin' invitations to the congregation
    stringin'
Up the road to old St. Michael's, on the blessed
    day of prayer.
You might seek the boundin' gait of him in any
    youth or maiden
With the rhythmic pulse of summer, and in vain
    would be the search;
Steppin' on with fine importance, like a general
    paradin'
In his Sunday regimentals, comes the Pillar of the
    Church.

There be mighty ones a-comin', most bedazzlin' in
    their dressin'—
Silken, swishin', sweepin' garments, gold and gems
    so fine to see;

There be homely ones in "fine clothes" with no
    less assurance pressin',
And the candid smell of moth-balls clingin' round
    the finery,
There be strength and fashion flauntin' this their
    hour above their neighbours;
Little faded beaded bonnets droppin' slowly to the
    rear;
Aged achin' shoulders stoopin' 'neath the trials and
    the labours,
Hobblin' on and crutch-supported where they
    hastened yester-year.

But there's somethin' in the step of him, there's
    somethin' in his bearin',
Somethin' haughty-like and scornful, as he paces
    to the fore,
Somethin' swellin' out responsive to the flattery of
    the starin',
Of the little groups discussin' parish gossip round
    the door.
What if through the workin' week-days, fame his
    humble labours scornin',
He is just a common mortal whom the stains of
    toil besmirch,
Whose opinions matter nothin'—here he is the
    Blessed Mornin'
In his Sunday regimentals,—and the Pillar of the
    Church.

Ay, the Pillar of the Church is he, and woe to
    them who'd doubt him;
Faith, he'd put them to the right-about, and face
    them to the rear,
For it's never parish-priest there's been could carry
    on without him,
Since St. Michael's been a parish church—it's goin'
    on fifty year.
Don't we see him time and time again, the chest
    of him expandin',
Superintendin' things that matter not, and things
    that matter much?
Don't we see him with "the gentlemen," the officer
    commandin',
Every Christmas Day and Easter writin' down the
    names and such?

Ain't he present all occasions when there's grave
    deliberatin'
On important parish matters at the school or
    presbyt'ry?
With the eyes of him a-blinkin' and the wisdom
    radiatin'—
He, the sole survivin' member of the first church
    "Komitee"?
And maintainin' which distinction, don't it make
    stonewallin' sweeter?—
And a heap of "argyfyin' " cannot shift him from
    his perch—

Don't he tell them how they did things in the time
    of Father Peter?
Faith, he shows 'em there's a kick left in the Pillar
    of the Church.

Sure the Pillar of the Church it was that saved the
    situation,
"With the whole of 'em agin him," as I've often
    heard him tell;
'Twas he "seen the danger comin'," he that "med
    the suggestation."
He that "druv 'em to their rat-holes," where he
    shook 'em good and well.
He's the Pillar of the Church, bedad, and never shy
    or shrinkin',
Nor afraid to be upstandin' his opinions for to
    state.
Times the priest he's flabbergasted; once he set the
    bishop thinkin';
That he did, Man—"ups and ats" him, "lets him
    have it purty straight."

Och, 'twould do you good to hear him, with an
    "audjunce" round him gawkin',
Tell of openin's here and "big days," puttin'
    modern feats to scorn;
And the banquets and the speeches, and the "Arrah,
    don't be talkin',
Sure the half of them that's livin' now don't know
    that they are born."

G

And the priests he knew by dozens, and the
    strugglin' and the strivin',
And the failure starin' at 'em, had he left 'em in
    the lurch;
Times and times he travelled with 'em, and
    "tremenjus" was the drivin'—
Pshaw, a hundred miles was larkin' to the Pillar of
    the Church.

Ay, the Pillar of the Church is he; and still at Mass
    or meetin'
There's the crabbéd old bald head of him, con-
    spicuous to the view.
And at answerin' up the prayers betimes the voice
    of him competin'
With its thunders shames the thin attempts of
    others in the pew;
See the poisonous little face of him at Cooney's
    baby screechin',
And the twistin' and the glarin', and then listenin'
    like a hare
While His Reverence reads the notices—but plottin'
    through the preachin'
For to get a kick at Murphy's dog, that's ramblin'
    everywhere.

Times and times he's "riz their dander"—every
    member up agin him—
And the jealous call him "Curate," while the
    flippant call him "Pope";

But he doesn't care a "thraneen," for "the venyum"
    isn't in him,
Happy just to be a leader where the lesser spirits
    grope,
Priests have come and priests have left us; change
    has blown from every quarter;
Him alone the grim marauder ne'er has chanced on
    in the search;
But we'd miss him were he taken, as we'd miss the
    holy water—
He's the feature of the Sunday, is the Pillar of the
    Church.

TEDDO WELLS, DECEASED

Times I think I'm not the man—
  Must be some mistake.
Me among the also ran?
  Cute and wideawake!
Old and beat and crotchety—
  Sixty-five, at least—
Knockin' round the presbytery,
  Groomin' for the priest,
Choppin' wood, and ringin' bells,
Dodgin' work and takin' spells!
Me all right, one Ed'ard Wells
  (Late Teddo Wells, deceased)—
Wheelin' barrows round the yard,
Gammon to be workin' hard,
  A-groomin' for the priest!

Trainin' prads was Teddo's game;
  Made a tidy bit.
Everybody knew the name,
  Teddo Wells was "It."
Bought that bit of property
  (Value since increased),
Gettin' on tremendously,
  Married by the priest.

Papers full of Teddo Wells,
Trainin' horses for the swells;
Since redooced to ringin' bells
   (Teddo Wells, deceased)
Shinin' boots and learnin' sense,
Nailin' palin's on the fence,
   A-groomin' for the priest.

Lost that bit of property,
   Ended up in smoke—
Too much "Jimmie Hennessy"—
   Down, and stony-broke.
Used to think he knew the game
   Till they had him fleeced.
"Mud" is this 'ere hero's name,
   Workin' for the priest—
Unbeknown to sports and swells;
They've no time for Ed'ard Wells.
Up the spout and ringin' bells
   As "Teddo Wells, deceased";
Never noticed up the town,
Never asked to keep one down—
   Groomin' for the priest.

Times I stops a cove to chat,
   One as gamed and spieled;
Chips me in the curate's hat,
   "Six to four the field."

"What-o! Teddo Wells," sez he,
  "Him that horses leased,
Owned that bit of property,
  Groomin' for the priest?"
"Guessin' eggs and seen the shells;
Brains," sez I, "and breedin' tells,
This old gent is Ed'ard Wells,
  Late Teddo Wells, deceased.
Ringin' bells is Ed'ard's game,
Openin' doors and closin' same,
  Called 'groomin'' for the priest."

Never see a horse nohow,
  Just an old machine;
Always in a tearin' row
  With this Josephine.
Got an eye that makes you feel
  Well and truly p'liced,
Follerin' out upon your heels,
  A-goin' to tell the priest.
"Can't smoke here now, Ed'ard Wells,
That old pipe offensive smells;
Go and smoke outside," she yells.
  So Teddo Wells, deceased,
Him that once was in the boom,
Wood-heap has for smokin' room—
  A-groomin' for the priest.

Times I says it's all a joke
  Someone's puttin' up;
Me dead-beat and stony-broke,
  Me that won a cup,

Owned that bit of property,
  Them good horses leased!
Kickin' round the presbytery
  A-groomin' for the priest!
Choppin' wood and ringin' bells,
Curby-hocked and takin' spells!
Me it is, one Ed'ard Wells,
  (Late Teddo Wells, deceased)
Smokin' hard and talkin' free
Of the man he used to be,
  And groomin' for the priest.

NORAH O'NEILL

That Norah O'Neill is a sthreel,*
And I'm talking the way that I feel,
With her dowdy old hat, and her hair pasted flat,
And her skirt bobbing after her heel;
And there to the church she will steal,
And under the lamp she will kneel
When confessions are done, and there's never a
    one
To be heard but that Norah O'Neill.

It annoys the priest's man a great deal,
And it makes every one boogathiel
At him scraping the floor, yes, and rattlin' the
    door
Just to hurry my lady O'Neill.
But there she will squat on her heel,
While over the forms he will steal;
He would put out the light, and close up for the
    night—
But he can't for that keershuch O'Neill.

---

* Slattern; also spelt streel. In the next verse boogathiel
means uncomfortable, and keershuch much the same as
sthreel.

I believe (and I talk as I feel)
When there at the Judgment we kneel,
And, each in his place, is the whole human race—
One half to be sent to the deil—
That, just as they're setting the seal,
A dust-cloud a glance will reveal
At the end of the day, Jerusalem way;
And you'll find 'twill be Norah O'Neill,
With her skirt bobbing after her heel,
And we'll have to go through the whole business
    anew;
Och, Norah O'Neill is a sthreel.

THE PRESBYT'RY DOG

Now of all the old sinners in mischief immersed,
  From the ages of Gog and Magog,
At the top of the list, from the last to the first,
And by every good soul in the parish accursed,
  Is that scamp of a Presbyt'ry Dog.

He's a hairy old scoundrel as ugly as sin,
  He's a demon that travels incog.,
With a classical name, and an ignorant grin,
And a tail, by the way, that is scraggy and thin,
  And the rest of him merely a dog.

He is like a young waster of fortune possessed,
  As he rambles the town at a jog;
For he treats the whole world as a sort of a jest,
While the comp'ny he keeps—well, it must be
      confessed
  It's unfit for a Presbyt'ry Dog.

He is out on the street at the sound of a fight,
  With the eyes on him standing agog,
And the scut of a tail—well, bedad, it's a fright;
Faith, you'd give him a kick that would set him
      alight,
  But you can't with the Presbyt'ry Dog.

His rotundity now to absurdity runs,
   Like a blackfellow gone to the grog;
For the knowing old shaver the presbyt'ry shuns
When it's time for a meal, and goes off to the
      nuns,
   Who're deceived in the Presbyt'ry Dog.

When he follows the priest to the bush, there is
      war.
   He inspects the whole place at a jog,
And he puts on great airs and fine antics galore,
While he chases the sheep till we're after his
      gore,
   Though he may be the Presbyt'ry Dog.

'Twas last Sunday a dog in the church went
      ahead
   With an ill-bred and loud monologue,
And the priest said some things that would shiver
      the dead,
And I'm with him in every last word that he
      said—
   Ah, but wait—'twas the Presbyt'ry Dog.

TANGMALANGALOO

The bishop sat in lordly state and purple cap
 sublime,
And galvanized the old bush church at Confirm-
 ation time;
And all the kids were mustered up from fifty miles
 around,
With Sunday clothes, and staring eyes, and ignor-
 ance profound.
Now was it fate, or was it grace, whereby they
 yarded too
An overgrown two-storey lad from Tangmalan-
 galoo?

A hefty son of virgin soil, where nature has her
 fling,
And grows the trefoil three feet high and mats it
 in the spring;
Where mighty hills uplift their heads to pierce the
 welkin's rim,
And trees sprout up a hundred feet before they
 shoot a limb;

There everything is big and grand, and men are
    giants too–
But Christian Knowledge wilts, alas, at Tangmalan-
    galoo.

The bishop summed the youngsters up, as bishops
    only can;
He cast a searching glance around, then fixed upon
    his man.
But glum and dumb and undismayed through every
    bout he sat;
He seemed to think that he was there, but wasn't
    sure of that.
The bishop gave a scornful look, as bishops some-
    times do,
And glared right through the pagan in from
    Tangmalangaloo.

"Come, tell me, boy," his lordship said in crushing
    tones severe,
"Come, tell me why is Christmas Day the greatest
    of the year?
"How is it that around the world we celebrate that
    day
"And send a name upon a card to those who're far
    away?
"Why is it wandering ones return with smiles and
    greetings, too?"
A squall of knowledge hit the lad from Tang-
    malangaloo.

He gave a lurch which set a-shake the vases on the
  shelf,
He knocked the benches all askew, up-ending of
  himself.
And oh, how pleased his lordship was, and how he
  smiled to say,
"That's good, my boy. Come, tell me now; and
  what is Christmas Day?"
The ready answer bared a fact no bishop ever
  knew—
"It's the day before the races out at Tangma-
  langaloo."

THE ALTAR-BOY

Now McEvoy was altar-boy
  As long as I remember;
He was, bedad, a crabbéd lad,
  And sixty come December.
Faith, no one dared to "interfare"
  In things the which concernin'
'Twas right and just to him to trust
  Who had the bit o' learnin'
To serve the priest; and here at least
  He never proved defaulter;
So, wet or dry, you could rely
  To find him on the Altar.

The acolyte in surplice white
  Some admiration rouses:
But McEvoy was altar-boy
  In "Sund'y coat-'n-trouses."
And out he'd steer, the eye severe
  The depths behind him plumbin',
In dread, I wot (he once was "cot"),
  The priest might not be comin':

Then, stepping slow on heel and toe,
 No more he'd fail or falter,
But set likewise with hands and eyes
 He'd move about the Altar.

A master-stroke of other folk
 Might start the opposition,
And some, mebbe, in jealousy
 Bedoubt their erudition;
But McEvoy was altar-boy
 And, spite of all their chattin',
It "put the stuns" on lesser ones
 To hear him run the Latin.
And faith, he knew the business through,
 The rubrics and the psalter;
You never met his "aikals" yet
 When servin' on the Altar.

The priest, indeed, might take the lead
 By right of Holy Orders,
But McEvoy was altar-boy,
 And just upon the borders.
So sermons dry he'd signify
 With puckered brows behoovin',
An', if you please, at homilies
 He'd nod the head approvin';
And all the while a cute old smile
 Picked out the chief defaulter;
Faith, wet or dry, the crabbéd eye
 Would "vet" you from the Altar.

AT CASEY'S AFTER MASS

There's a weather-beaten sign-post where the track
    turns towards the west,
Through the tall, white, slender timber, in the land
    I love the best.
Short its message is—"To Casey's"—for it points
    the road to Casey's;
And my homing heart goes bushwards on an idle
    roving quest,
Down the old, old road contented, o'er the gum-
    leaves crisp and scented,
Where a deft hand splashed the purple on the big
    hill's sombre crest.
Ah, it's long, long years and dreary, many, many
    steps and weary,
Back to where the lingering dew of morn bedecked
    the barley-grass,
When I watched the wild careering of the neigh-
    bours through the clearing
Down that sweet bush track to Casey's, o'er the
    paddock down to Casey's;
Spending Sunday down at Casey's after Mass.

H

For, as soon as Mass was over, round the church
    they swarmed like bees,
Filled their pipes and duly lit them, brushed the
    dust from off their knees;
Then they'd "ready-up" for Casey's—self-invited
    down to Casey's—
Harness horses for the women with a bushman's
    careless ease.
With a neat spring to the saddle, soon would start
    the wild skedaddle,
Passing gigs and traps and buggies packed as tight
    as they could squeeze;
Hearts as buoyant as a feather in the mellow
    autumn weather,
While the noisy minahs cheered to see the glad
    procession pass—
All the Regans and the Ryans, and the whole mob
    of O'Briens
Bringing up the rear to Casey's—in the Shandrydan
    to Casey's—
Spending Sunday down at Casey's after Mass.

Past the kitchen door they rattled and they took
    the horses out;
While the women went inside at once, the men-
    folk hung about
Round the stable down at Casey's, waiting dinner
    down at Casey's;
And they talked about the Government, and
    blamed it for the drought,

Sitting where the sunlight lingers, picking splinters
    from their fingers,
Settling all the problems of the world beyond a
    chance of doubt.
From inside there came the bustle of the cheerful
    wholesome hustle,
As dear old Mrs. Casey tried all records to sur-
    pass;
Oh, there's many a memory blesses her sweet
    silver-braided tresses;
They were "lovely" down at Casey's—always
    joking down at Casey's—
Spending Sunday down at Casey's after Mass.

So they called us in to dinner, five-and-twenty
    guests—and more—
At the longest kitchen-table ever stood upon a
    floor.
There was plenty down at Casey's—ay, an open
    house was Casey's,
Where the neighbour and his missus never, never
    passed the door;
Where they counted kindly giving half the joy
    and pride of living
And the seasons came full-handed, and the angels
    blessed the store;
While the happy Laughing Mary flitted round us
    like a fairy.
And the big, shy boys stopped business, and looked
    up to watch her pass—

Ah, but when she caught them staring at the
    ribbons she was wearing!
Well, they spilled their tea at Casey's—on the good
    clean cloth at Casey's—
Spending Sunday down at Casey's after Mass.

Then the reckless feats of daring, and the bush-
    man's fierce delight
When the brumby squealed and rooted, and the
    saddle-girths were tight!
They could ride 'em down at Casey's—stick like
    plasters down at Casey's—
When they noticed Mary looking, they would go
    with all their might;
Ho! they belted, and they clouted, and they yelled,
    and whooped, and shouted,
"Riding flash" to "ketch" the ladies, spurring,
    flogging, left and right!
And the lad with manners airy risked his neck for
    Laughing Mary
When he summoned all his courage up a rival to
    surpass;
Oh, the fun went fast and faster, as he landed in
    disaster
In the puddle-hole at Casey's—with his brand new
    suit at Casey's—
Spending Sunday down at Casey's after Mass.

Hoary, hale, bewhiskered veterans, perched like
    mopokes in a row,
Out of danger on the top-rail, gave advice to those
    below;

They were wonders down at Casey's, were the
    old men at the Caseys'—
They're the boys could ride the "bad 'uns" in the
    days of long ago!
Faith, and old man Casey told 'em of a way he
    had to hold 'em.
Man, "the deuce an outlaw thrun him," when he
    "got a proper show";
Ay, and each man "upped and showed 'em" how
    he "handled 'em, an' rode 'em"—
Pshaw! there never was a native these old riders
    could outclass.
Once again they were "among 'em," and they
    "roped 'em" and they "slung 'em"
On the stockyard fence at Casey's—smoking,
    "pitchin'," down at Casey's—
Spending Sunday down at Casey's after Mass.

Hard and cold is youth to fancies which around
    the old men cling;
So they left them perched upon the rail to swap
    their vapouring,
Took a seat inside at Casey's, on the good chairs
    at the Caseys';
While the Caseys' new piano made the old house
    rock and ring.
There their mild eyes stared and glistened, as they
    sat around and listened
To the tuneful little ditties Laughing Mary used to
    sing;

There they rubbed their chins and reckoned that
    to no one was she second—
"Cripes, she'd sing the blooming head off any
    singer in her class!"
And the banter and the laughter when the chorus
    hit the rafter!
It was "great" to be at Casey's—healthy, wholesome
    fun at Casey's—
Spending Sunday down at Casey's after Mass.

There was something in the old life which I cannot
    quite forget;
There are happy golden memories that hover
    round me yet—
Something special down at Casey's, in that won-
    derland of Casey's,
Where the crowfoot and the clover spread a
    downy coverlet,
Where the trees seemed always greener, where the
    life of man was cleaner,
And the joys that grew around us shed no leaves
    of brown regret.
Oh, the merry, merry party! oh, the simple folk
    and hearty,
Who can fling their cares behind them, and forget
    them while they pass
Simple lives and simple pleasure never stinted in
    the measure.
There was something down at Casey's, something
    clean and good at Casey's—
Spending Sunday down at Casey's after Mass.

Passed and gone that old bush homestead where
    the hours too swiftly flew;
Silent now the merry voices of the happy friends
    I knew;
We have drifted far from Casey's. All deserted
    now is Casey's—
Just a lone brick chimney standing, and a garden-
    tree or two.
Still the minahs love to linger where the sign-post
    points the finger
Down the bush track winding westward where the
    tall white timber grew.
But the big hill seems to wonder why the ties are
    snapped asunder,
Why the neighbours never gather, never loiter as
    they pass;
Yet a tear-stained thought beseeming comes along
    and sets me dreaming
That I'm back again at Casey's, with the old, old
    friends at Casey's;
Spending Sunday down at Casey's after Mass.

ST. PATRICK'S DAY

'Tis the greatest splash of sunshine right through
all my retrospection
  On the days when fairies brought me golden
  dreams without alloy,
When I gazed across the gum-trees round about
the old selection
  To the big things far beyond them, with the
  yearning of a boy.

Drab the little world we lived in; like the sheep,
in slow procession
  Down the track along the mountain, went the
  hours upon their way,
Bringing hopes and idle longings that could only
find expression
  In the riot of our bounding hearts upon St.
  Patrick's Day.

There were sports in Casey's paddock, and the
neighbours would assemble
  On the flat below the homestead, where the
  timber fringed the creek;

With Australian skies above them, and Australian
    trees a-tremble
  And the colours of the autumn set in hat and
    hair and cheek.

Mighty things were done at Casey's; mighty bouts
    anticipated
  Made the Sunday church-door topic for a month
    ahead at least;
On the cheerless Sundays after, with misguided
    hope deflated,
  We explained away our failures as we waited for
    the priest.

So when morning Mass was over, it was trot and
    break and canter
  Helter-skelter down to Casey's, banging, pound-
    ing all the way,
And the greetings flung in Irish, and the flood of
    Celtic banter,
  And the hectic flush of racial pride upon St.
    Patrick's Day.

Everywhere was emerald flashing from the buggies,
    traps, and jinkers,
  There was green in every garment, and a splash
    in every hat,
In the bows upon the cart-whips, in the ribbons on
    the winkers,
  In the wealth of woven carpet neath the gums
    on Casey's Flat.

There the new dress faced the critics, and the little
    beaded bonnet
  And the feather flowing freely like a sapling in
    a gale;
And "himself" inside his long black coat that bore
    a bulge upon it
  Where for twelve forgotten months its weight
    had hung upon the nail;

And the "splather" of a necktie only once a year
    paraded,
  And the scarf that came from Ireland, "ere a one
    of you were born,"
And the treasured bunch of shamrock—old and
    withered now, and faded,
  Blessed by every tear that stained it since the
    cruel parting morn.

Mighty things were done at Casey's. Men of solid
    reputation,
  Ringing bells and giving orders, kept the pro-
    gramme moving by;
And they made you sickly conscious of your
    humble situation
  When they glared upon your meanness with a
    cold official eye.

Every "maneen" with a broken voice and backers
    there beside him,
  And his socks outside his breeches, was a hero
    in his way;

Every nag around the country with a raw bush lad
    astride him
  Was a racehorse with an Irish name upon St.
    Patrick's Day.

Oh, the cheering that betokened those I knew so
    well competing,
  With their long legs throwing slip-knots, and
    the look of men in pain—
Put me back into the reach-me-downs, and let me
    hear the greeting,
  Set me loose in Casey's paddock, where I'd be a
    boy again!

Yes, 'twas good to be a pilgrim in a world that
    held such wonders,
  Though eternal bad behaviour put me neath
    parental ban,
Though the staring, and the wandering, and a
    score of general blunders
  Got me gaoled behind the taffrail of the Old
    Mass Shandrydan.

"Yerra, Johnnie, stop that gawkin." Is it—with the
    pulses pumping,
  And the little heart high-stepping to the music of
    the drum—
Is it "stop it," with a something in the young blood
    madly thumping
  With a foreword of the purpose of the pregnant
    years to come?

Mighty things were done at Casey's. Mighty
    impulse was behind them,
  'Twas the sacred spark enkindled that was
      burning to the bone;
Never yet were men more loyal to the holy ties
    that bind them,
  And the love they gave their country made me
    conscious of my own.

Never yet were men more loyal. Be they met in
    thousands teeming,
  Be they gathered down at Casey's with their
    kindred and their kind;
They are marching on for Ireland, with the beau-
    teous vision gleaming
  Of the altar-fires of Freedom in the land they
    left behind.

Not a torch was ever lighted at a tomb where
    Freedom slumbered,
  But it smouldered—grimly smouldered—till the
    stone was rolled away;
When it flashed across the half-light, rallying
    rocket glares unnumbered,
  Like the spangled blades of morning that bespeak
    the march of day.

Not a voice was ever lifted, but an echo never
    dying
  Flung the slogan once repeated when the hand
    was on the gun;

Though the prophet tongue was ashes, came the
    conquering banners flying
  With a dazzling watchword flashing, blazing
    signals in the sun.

Yes, the world has ever seen it in its journey down
    the ages,
  Seen it writ in living scarlet in the blood that has
    been shed;
And a hand re-writes the head-line deep across the
    lurid pages,
  When the stricken, fearless living meet the
    deathless, martyred dead.

Thrills a leaping thought within me, when I see a
    land around me
  That has never seen the foeman's steel, nor heard
    the foeman's shot,
At whose shrine I lit the tapers, when her witching
    sweetness bound me
  With an iron vow of service of a pulsing pride
    begot;

To that big free land I've given all the love that
    courses through me;
  That her hands have rocked my cradle stirs my
    heart in every beat.
An Australian, ay, Australian—oh, the word is
    music to me,
  And the craven who'd deny her would I spurn
    beneath my feet.

Thrills the thought that, did the traitor stretch a
    tainted hand to foil her,
  Did I see her flag of silver stars a tattered thing
      and torn,
Did I see her trampled, breathless, neath the shod
    heel of the spoiler,
  And her bleeding wounds a byword, and her
      name a thing of scorn,

There would flash the living bayonets in the strong
    hands of my brothers,
  And the blood that coursed for nationhood,
      through all the years of pain,
In the veins of patriot fathers and of Little Irish
    Mothers
  Would be hot as hissing lava streams to thrill the
      world again.

THE CAREYS

Their new house stood just off the road,
    A fine big brick two-storey,
All gabled, tiled, and porticoed,
    To flaunt its owners' glory.
We never had, to tell the truth,
    At Carey's door alighted,
We had good reasons too, forsooth—
    We hadn't been invited.
But down to Mass we passed the gate,
    And passed it, too, returning,
And hid away in mien sedate
    The grievance in us burning.
But in the Old Mass Shandrydan—
    Well, envy little varies—
We heard "herself" and her good man
    Discourse about the Careys:

"Wisha, that big house of Carey's with its power
    of fal-de-daries."
    "Faith, he's in the bank to build it, so I hear the
    people say."
"It will break him now to clear it; and it's grieved
    I am to hear it;
    Wisha, I wouldn't be in Carey's boots to-day!"

They came here in the early days,
   And settled down as neighbours;
With tilted carts and bullock-drays
   They shared our griefs and labours.
We tramped it to the old bush school,
   In fine or rainy weather;
And there upon the dunce's stool
   We took our knocks together.
But now they stood for "class" among
   Our little congregation;
And, as they passed us by, they flung
   Mere scraps of toleration.
And sometimes down to Mass they'd bring
   Fine strangers holidaying,
Who laughed and gushed at everything
   Within their orbit straying.
By soft white hands and modish gowns
   They sought the world to measure,
And seemed to think our reach-me-downs
   Were staged to give them pleasure.
And, faith, it set the tongues a-wag
   And entertained the flippants
To see the fifteen-guinea bag
   That held the little "thrippence,"
While in the church they plied the fan
   And practised like vagaries;
So in the Old Mass Shandrydan
   We gave it to the Careys:

"Wisha, did you see the Careys? They're the high-
       falutin fairies."
   "Tell me, who were them play-actors there that
       had so much to say?"
"Och, the antics and the wrigglin', and the goin's-
       on and gigglin'—
   Wisha, did you see the Careys there to-day!"

They sometimes drove a spanking pair,
    Which brought them speed and honour;
They sometimes drove a pacing-mare
    With straps and pads upon her;
They covered us with clouds of dust,
    As thick as we could wear it;
And we could plod, as needs we must,
    And keep the faith and bear it.
When skies were blue and days were bright,
    And leaf and bud were sprouting,
They came to Mass in splendour dight,
    To make a Sunday's outing;
But when the morn was blank with storm
    And winter blasts complaining,
The Careys kept devotion warm
    Beside their fire remaining.
So, while the chilling torrents ran
    And soaked our best figaries,
Within the Old Mass Shandrydan
    We pummelled at the Careys:

I

"Wisha, where were all the Careys? Sure the rain
    might melt the fairies!"
  "Faith, and if it was the races then, they
    wouldn't stop away."
"That'd be another story; there they'd be in all
    their glory—
  Wisha, what could keep them all from Mass
    to-day!"

And when we held the big bazaar—
  A fine and lively meeting—
And people came from near and far,
  In buoyant zeal competing,
'Twas rush and gush and fulsomeness
  And Careys superintending;
They raced about in evening dress,
  And deftly dodged the spending.
We might have been in Amsterdam,
  Or somewhere out in Flanders;
We sold some tickets for "the ham,"
  And stalked about like ganders.
So when we gathered up the clan,
  And sought our distant eyries,
Within the Old Mass Shandrydan
  We blazed it at the Careys:

"Wisha, did you see the Careys, like some wild
    things from the prairies?"
  "Faith, I never met 'the bate' of that for many
    'n many a day."

"Sure it's pounds we would have taken with them
    tickets for the bacon,
  If them thuckeens* of the Careys were not
    always in the way."

And when the little choir we had
  In tender hope was springing,
And nervous lass and awkward lad
  Were mobilized for singing,
We all went down our own to hear,
  As holy triumph crowned them,
But Careys sailed in shrill and clear,
  And silenced all around them;
Our Nellie's range they quite outran,
  And even Laughing Mary's;
So in the Old Mass Shandrydan
  We pitched into the Careys:

"Wisha, did you hear the Careys? Don't they think
    they're fine canaries?"
  "Yerra, wouldn't you think they'd hold the
    tongues, and let the people pray!"
"Faith, my head is all a-reelin' from them Careys
    and their squealin'—
  Wisha, did you hear them shoutin' there
    to-day!"

The angels, in their peaceful skies
  Through starry paddocks straying,
Must sometimes smile with kindly eyes
  To see the tricks we're playing.

---

* Celtic for "flapper."

Now rosy-cheeked and smart and fair
  Was Carey's youngest daughter;
And lo, our Morgan did his hair
  With mutton-fat and water;
But days and days the lovers spent
  On thorns (and roses) treading,
Till down to Carey's house we went,
  Invited to the wedding.
For life's a fine comedian,
  Whose programme shifts and varies,
And in the Old Mass Shandrydan
  We smoodged a bit to Careys:

"Wisha, now we'll see the Careys in their weddin'
    fal-de-daries!"
  "Faith, I mind the time the Careys slep' beneath
    their bullock-dray."
"Sure, I wouldn't hurt their feelin's, though I never
    liked their dealin's;
  "An' if just to please poor Morgan, I'll be nice
    to them to-day."

WHEN OLD MAN CAREY DIED

A night of wind and driving rain,
  No light on land or sky—
The sharp squalls shook the window-pane
  And scurried loudly by,

When sped abroad the message stern
  On cantering hoofbeats borne
That old man Carey "took a turn,"
  And might not see the morn.

What though debarred from Carey's set,
  What though 'twas plainly seen
The new house and its etiquette
  Had made a gulf between,

What matter if they passed us by
  And scorned us heretofore—
We could not spurn a neighbour's cry
  When trouble found his door.

So through the dark, a swinging light
  Beneath the axle tied,
The neighbours braved the stormy night
  When old man Carey died.

All blank was Carey's new brick place
  As, entering through the gloom
With noiseless step, we just might trace
  Within a darkened room

The purple stole that purifies,
  The old wife's stricken head,
The Carey girls, with swollen eyes,
  All kneeling round the bed—

We'd move the world to help them, then:
  Our feuds were laid aside,
For all were neighbours once again
  When old man Carey died.

And, when he'd paid the debt perforce
  That every man must pay,
We came again with hearse and horse
  To bear him on his way.

We left behind the new brick place
  So strangely silent now,
The death-mask on its staring face,
  The ashes on its brow;

Slow straggling down the winding road,
  Past ripening crops a-sweep
Which old man Carey's hands had sowed
  But other hands would reap,

With slap and tap of unshod heels
  We followed one by one,
And fifty sets of idling wheels
  Were twinkling in the sun.

With many a tale of deeds unguessed,
  Deeds of the early years,
We brought him to his long, long rest
  Among the pioneers.

THE PARTING ROSARY

They have brought the news, my darlin', that I've
    waited for so long.
Faith, 'twas little news they brought me; every
    story, every song
That I've heard since you enlisted seemed to bear
    the one refrain,
Till the whole world used to tell me that you'd
    never come again.
They've been cruel times, alannah, since you left
    us for the fight,
Potterin' dazed-like all the daytime, thinkin',
    thinkin' through the night;
Yerra, what's the use complainin', when the world
    is all amiss,
When the hopin' and the strivin' ever come to
    dust like this.
'Twas the green months when you left me; now
    the brown, brown months have come,
Stand the ripe crops in the paddocks, but the
    harvesters are dumb.
There'll be flowers again in plenty, and a carpet
    o'er the plain—
Oh, it's hard you won't be comin' when the green
    months come again!

Still, I'm thankful, oh, I'm thankful for one golden
    memory,
That the last time spent together was to say The
    Rosary.
Don't you mind it, boy? we said it in my own
    room there beyond,
Where I have the little altar where your early
    prayers you conned,
By the statue that I cherish of the Holy Mother
    fair,
With the blue cloak round her shoulders, and her
    white hands crossed in prayer.
They were singin' in the parlour, them that came
    to say good-bye;
And they sang their gay songs to me—och, I knew
    the reason why!
They are always kind in trouble in this big warm-
    hearted land;
Ah, but their way wasn't my way, and they
    mightn't understand.
So I lit the little candles, and I beckoned you
    away,
And you came—God bless you for it, boy—the
    partin' prayer to say.
Ay, the partin' Rosary, darlin'—I can see you
    kneelin' there,
With your big broad shoulders bendin', and your
    hands joined on the chair,

And your man's voice like an organ rollin' out its
    soul apart—
Och, to-night, boy, in my dreamin' it is dronin' in
    my heart.
Yes, we said it with the music strummin' ragtime
    songs throughout,
Just our two selves there together, answerin' t'other
    turn about.
'Tis a quare, quare world, alannah, when the storm
    can work its stress
On the strong limb, while the withered leaf is left
    in loneliness.
"Lay your treasure up in Heaven," for there's
    nothing here below;
Och, we Irish mothers learned it in the old land
    long ago!
Short life's springtime with its blossom; and it
    comes not back again,
Only haggard trees in winter stretchin' naked limbs
    in pain.
Oh, I'm thankin' God, my bouhal,* though the
    achin's in my breast,
'Twas He took you from me, darlin', and He
    knoweth what is best:
And His Holy Mother Mary, with her Baby on
    her knee,
Sure she lost Him in His manhood, for He died at
    thirty-three.

---

* Boy; also spelt bouchal.

There's a numbin' in my heart, boy; like a cold,
    cold hand it grips—
Oh, I'm thankful that we parted with the Rosary
    on your lips.
It has ever been my refuge; it has been my hope
    and stay,
Been my hymn of sweet thanksgivin' for what good
    there came my way.
It has been my only comfort when the heart was
    sick and sore,
When the bad days past the countin' flung their
    troubles round my door.
I was taught it by my mother; ay, and when we
    crossed the sea
For to seek the gold we never found—the old man
    there and me
(Sure he stood six feet and higher then, and coal-
    black was his hair—
Och, you'd never know 'twas him at all, that bent
    old man in there)—
We have said it in the slab hut, strong and clear in
    flood and drought,
Just our two selves there together "answerin' up"
    and "givin' out."
We have said it by the cradle, we have said it by
    the cot;
When the babes the angels brought us made us
    happy in our lot,

When the house was full of childer, and the pride
     of livin' glowed,
Och, we said it till the neighbours heard us, passin'
     on the road.
But ye've gone and left me lonely; one by one, my
     doves, ye flew;
One by one the circle's dwindled, till the Rosary's
     said by two—
Said by two old husky voices, old and weak and
     wearin' out,
Just our two old selves together, answerin' t'other
     turn about.
Sure it won't be long, alannah, till the troubled sea
     is calm,
And the beads drop from my fingers, and they bind
     them on my arm.
You would tease me with the "trimmin's" in the
     dear days that are dead,
There's another trimmin' now, boy, every time the
     Rosary's said.
But there won't be many Rosaries, for the singin's
     in my ears
And the Holy Mother's beckonin'—I can see her
     through my tears.
These old feet have done their journey, better leave
     them restin', then;
They will bring me to the hill-side ere the green
     months come again.

Sure I'll tread the House of Glory, where the soul
    is free from harm,
And you'll know 'tis me, alannah, by the Rosary
    on my arm.

OWNERLESS

He comes when the gullies are wrapped in the
      gloaming
  And limelights are trained on the tops of the
      gums,
To stand at the sliprails, awaiting the homing
  Of one who marched off to the beat of the
      drums.

So handsome he looked in the putties and khaki,
  Light-hearted he went like a youngster to
      play;
But why comes he never to speak to his Darkie,
  Around at the rails at the close of the day?

And why have the neighbours foregathered so
      gently,
  Their horses a-doze at the fence in a row?
And what are they talking of, softly, intently?
  And why are the women-folk lingering so?

One hand, soft and small, that so often caressed
      him,
  Was trembling just now as it fondled his
      head;

But what was that trickling warm drop that
    distressed him?
  And what were those heart-broken words that
    she said?

Ne'er brighter the paddocks that bushmen re-
    member
  The green and the gold and the pink have dis-
    played,
When Spring weaves a wreath for the brows of
    September,
  Enrobed like a queen, and a-blush like a maid.

The gums are a-shoot and the wattles a-cluster,
  The cattle are roaming the ranges astray;
But why are they late with the hunt and the
    muster?
  And why is the black horse unsaddled to-day?

Hard by at the station the training commences,
  In circles they're schooling the hacks for the
    shows;
The high-mettled hunters are sent at the fences,
  And satins and dapples the brushes disclose.

Sound-winded and fit and quite ready is Darkie,
  Impatient to strip for the sprint and the flight;
But what can be keeping the rider in khaki?
  And why does the silence hang heavy to-night?

Ah, surely he'll come, when the waiting is
  ended,
  To fly the stiff fences and take him in hand,
Blue-ribboned once more, and three-quarters
  extended,
  Hard-held for the cheers from the fence and the
  stand.

Still there on the cross-beam the saddle hangs
  idle,
  The cobweb around the loose stirrup is spun;
The rust's on the spurs, and the dust on the
  bridle,
  And gathering mould on the badges he won.

We'll take the old horse to the paddocks to-
  morrow,
  Where grasses are waving breast-high on the
  plain;
And there with the clean-skins we'll turn him in
  sorrow
  And muster him never, ah, never, again.

The bush bird will sing when the shadows are
  creeping
  A sweet plaintive note, soft and clear as a
  bell's—
Oh, would it might ring where the bush boy is
  sleeping,
  And colour his dreams by the far Dardanelles.

LAUGHING MARY

With cheeks that paled the rosy morn
　　She bounded o'er the heather,
And romped with us among the corn
　　When we were kids together.
Her mother's help, her mother's mate,
　　Her mother's darling daughter,
When riper mind and more sedate
　　The rapid years had brought her.
As pure as air from mountain snows,
　　As dainty as a fairy,
As fetching as the native rose,
　　And always—Laughing Mary.

A little mother round about,
　　The happy sunshine bringing—
You'd see her bustle in and out,
　　A-working and a-singing;
And then the soul of Casey's place,
　　The love, the light, the laughter,
When friendship showed its cheery face,
　　And music shook the rafter;

K

And many a lad went home to find
   A haunting sweet vagary
Was rambling softly through his mind
   Because of Laughing Mary.

But when the smiling stars were blurred,
   And someone's heart was bleeding,
She flew as flies the homing bird,
   With balms of comfort speeding.
An angel in a sweet disguise,
   She filled the measure over,
While tears stood sparkling in her eyes
   Like rain-drops on the clover;
And many a head bowed low to pray,
   Howe'er her skies might vary,
The years would bless her on her way
   And keep her Laughing Mary.

MORYAH

"Wisha, where is he goin' to now
  With the hat on the back of the poll,
And the hair of him curled on the brow,
  Like a millionaire out for a stroll?"
"Ar', Old Man, but he's yardin' the cow."
          "Moryah!*
  With the hat on the back of his poll?"

"There's the red heifer's calf in the lane,
  And the gray mare is mad for a bite,
And the dog up above on the chain
  Is shoutin' and bawlin' all night."
"Sure, Old Man, you're keownrawnin' again."
          "Moryah!
  And that Jim gallivantin' the night?"

"Yer', Old Man, but the head of him's young;
  And the chubby gossoon with the dart
Have the wits of him straightened and strung
  To the tune of the song in the heart,
With the lilt of it there on the tongue."
          "Moryah—
  And bad luck from the song in the heart!"

* Moryah is the Celtic equivalent of "I don't think!"

" 'Tis that Casey girl now have him caught,
    And her mother out baking the bread;
It is there she should be, so she ought,
    With the eyes dancing jigs in her head;
Faith, when I was a boy, sure we thought . . ."
        "Moryah!
  'Twas yourself had an eye in the head."

"Don't I mind the old days that are through,
    When a boy and a colleen afar
Felt the bound and the hurt of it too
    As they swung in a dream on a star—
Thiggim-thu,* my Old Man, thiggim-thu?"
        "Ouisha,
  Poor old woman, 'tis dreamin' you are."

---

* "Don't you understand?"

A STRANGER IN THE CHURCH

'Twas Callagan who jerked the thumb—
A mute, interrogating thumb—
   That set the people staring
At Casey's lot arriving late.
They had in tow a fashion-plate
In tailored garments up-to-date,
   And patent leathers wearing.
From heel to collar shining new
(His hair was like a poet's, too),
He went and sat in Casey's pew,
   His lofty manners airing.

'Twas Mrs. Cooney raised her veil—
A handsome, netted, spotted veil—
   To mop the perspiration;
And while she mopped, she took the chance
To shoot one sly enquiring glance
(Which trivial happy circumstance
   Escaped his observation).
And McEvoy, he stole a look,
The while he gravely moved the book,
And certain useful bearings took
   To help the situation.

'Twas Mac himself who told the yarn—
An unauthenticated yarn—
   While after Mass we waited,
Of bank account, and purse, and pelf
("But, faith, he was a pagan elf—
I never seen him bless himself
   Nor read his book," Mac stated).
So there and then we made a bid
To find his secret where 'twas hid;
We found out what his father did,
   And how he was related.

'Twas brother Jim made up his mind—
A calculating, jealous mind—
   That "that there toff" was courting.
He saw him smile when Mary spoke,
He watched him help with Mary's cloak,
And drive away with Mary's folk,
   At Mary's side disporting.
And Mary looked so coy and trim—
At least it seemed that way to Jim—
And this it was that rattled him,
   Each trifle misreporting.

TELL ME, WHAT'S A GIRL TO DO?

Tell me, what's a girl to do
    When the gossoons court and cozen?
Some have none and some have two,
    More can count a baker's dozen.
Mary, Mary, by and by,
    With the woman in you wakin',
Boundin' heart and laughin' eye,
    There'll be murder, no mistakin'.

Cornered sits each captive lad
    Gazin' vacant at the rafter,
Talkin' wisdom with your dad—
    Faith, it isn't him they're after.
Wisha, Mary, there you be
    Neat and sweet and fair and fetchin',
Heart-whole still and fancy-free!
    Yer', Acushla, but 'tis ketchin'.

One can give you gold galore;
    Life with gilded gauds he'd smother
One can give you something more,
    Love, that ne'er can love another.

Boundin' heart, and laughin' eye,
  In the twinklin' sunlight walkin';
Love, you tell me, passes by—
  Wisha, Mary, don't be talkin'.

THE WIREE'S SONG

The wiree sang that Christmas Day,
A rippling, limpid, liquid lay
   In clump and cover trilling;
On ripened grain and gleaming road
The molten, golden sunlight glowed,
   The lone land's rapture stilling.

And health and strength and youth and grace
Were gathered down at Casey's place
   In mirthful mood of madness;
While, hidden in the currajong,
The wiree sang his limpid song,
   Responsive to the gladness.

And Mary sparkled everywhere,
The sunlight weaving through her hair
   The colours of December;
Ah, two shall strive—but one shall win
And one shall feel the javelin
   'Twere poison to remember!

The silent bush that Christmas Day
In molten, golden sunlight lay,
   Nor bough nor leaf a-tremble;
All hushed and mute, it seemed asleep,
Or wrapped away in musings deep
   That sleep itself resemble.

One voice the outer spaces filled—
That lilting lay the wiree trilled,
   Like raptures of a lover,
"Wir-ree, Wir-ree, Itchong, Itchong"—
Then rippled through its liquid song,
   Leaf-hidden in the cover.

And one has seen the love arise
To shade the light of laughing eyes
   Like white clouds in December;
But one has felt the piercing pang
That thrilled the song the wiree sang—
   And he shall still remember.

WISHA, WHAT IS THE MATTER WITH JIM?

"Wisha, what is the matter with Jim, I dunno?
Is he right in the mind for this last week or so?
   Or has he come in for a station?
He is trapesin' around, and he's treadin' on air,
He is brushin' the clothes, and he's doin' the
         hair;
He is like a play-actor at times, I declare,
   And his antics they beggar creation.

"Like a sheep-killing dog he'll be vanishing quite,
If you leave him one moment get out of your
         sight,
   With the fire and the fever prevailin';
While his horse is worn down to the skin and the
         bone
From the hours that he keeps. If you let him
         alone,
To the Caseys' he'd canter across on his own,
   And tie himself up to the palin'."

There's a track, through the timber that rambles
      along,
And a cantering horse vamps the time to a song
    That the heart of a dreamer is singing.
There are bells for a wedding that ring in the
      breeze,
That sound in the grass that is brushing his
      knees;
And down in the crowfoot, and up in the trees
    They're ringing, and ringing, and ringing.

SAID THE WHITE-HAIRED PRIEST

Said the white-haired priest, "So the boy has
     come,
  And the old, old dreams are o'er you,
And you give no thought to the gray humdrum
  Of the world that lies before you!
'Tis a queer old world; 'tis a jumble wild
  Where the fairest hopes may smother;
Ay, and things are just as they seem, my child,
  To the likes of your fine old mother.

"Put the dreams one side; give your head a
     chance,
  For the heart discerns but poorly,
And it beats the time of a mad wild dance,
  When a lover has gripped it surely.
There is one wise heart in the wanton whirl,
  Though you find through life no other;
And it beats with a sober pulse, my girl,
  In the breast of your grand old mother.

"Let them paint fresh colours on vale and hill,
  Let them say new flowers bloom brighter;
'Tis the same old rut on the highway still
  Which she trod when her steps were lighter.

And the same old hopes that her way beguiled,
　　And the same old griefs,—no other,
Ah, they wait hard by for yourself, my child,
　　As they did for your poor old mother.

"On her tired breast shall you tell your tale
　　When the drifting doubts distress you;
You shall kneel to her in your bridal veil,
　　And no holier hands shall bless you.
Put your young bright head, with its wealth of
　　　　curl,
　　By that old white head of the other,
And entwine the gold with the gray, my girl,
　　By the side of your dear old mother.

"Though her eyes be weary and dim to-day,
　　In the shade of the dusk advancing
She sees the visions along the way
　　Where your young swift feet are dancing;
At your fond sweet dreams she has gently
　　　　smiled!—
　　Yes, and you will smile at another
When you see the tinsel and sham, my child,
　　With the eyes of your wise old mother.

"Then go to her side and your story tell
　　With its hopes and its fears completed:
She will understand, ah, she knows it well,
　　It is merely her own repeated.

She will fold you close, and the tides that swell
   In your bosoms shall choke and smother;
Oh, it's blessed indeed is the bride, my girl,
   When she kneels by a gray old mother."

HONEYMOONING FROM THE COUNTRY

To the rooms where I am dining in the glaring
    city's day
Come the happy honeymooners from the country
    far away,
Two days old, and very awkward as they wander
    straight ahead,
Much too careful lest the people should suspect
    them country-bred.
He's a well set-up young fellow; she's a dainty
    little bride;
And he follows where she leads him with the bush
    swing in his stride,
Makes himself at home—or tries to—with defiance
    in his stare,
Thinks he's in the old bush kitchen with his hat
    beneath the chair.
Every eye is turned upon them, and the kindly
    smiles that flit
O'er the faces of the diners seem to bless them
    where they sit;
But for me the past revives with thronging
    memories in its train,
And I'm thinking that it's Jim and Laughing Mary
    once again.

Don't I see it all before me? and I feel the mood
    is good—
There's the horse tied by the sliprails, and a hole
    worn where he stood;
There's the dreamer riding homewards while the
    same old fancies throng,
With the same old stars a-staring, and the same old
    lilting song.
There's the "talkin' matters over," "gettin' all
    arrangements straight,"
Mum and Dad in the committee for the fixing of
    the date;
Then the buggies and the jinkers at the church
    upon the hill,
And the ribbons and the garlands, and the flounces
    and the "frill";
There's the breakfast down at Mother's—oh, the
    planning o'er and o'er,
And the murder and the tearing that went on the
    day before!
Working double shifts and bustling—every female
    in demand—
Half the women of the parish round to lend a
    helping hand,
Offering loans to bridge the shortage of the cups
    and spoons, and then
Tying threads around the handles, so they'll know
    their own again;

L

Racing in and out and fussing, so to strike the
country dumb;

But they'll talk of Mary's wedding for a score of
years to come!

Yes, the breakfast down at Mother's—there's the
long, long table spread,

And a houseful of the neighbours with the old
priest at their head;

And the speeches—Lord, the speeches—hitting
hurdles every stride,

Full of awkward, heartfelt blessings for the bride-
groom and the bride;

And the lad himself "respondin'," when the cheers
had died away,

Shifting crumbs around the table in the worst
speech of the day.

Don't I see it all before me? and my heart and head
resent

All the smiles that patronize them, though they
may be kindly meant.

"Scent of gum-leaves!" 'Tis a byword in the city's
roar and push,

Where they do not know the greatness and the
kindness of the bush.

"Scent of gum-leaves," so they whisper. Oh, it
sweetens not the air

In the overcrowded city, for the spirit is not
there.

Scent of gum-leaves to be scoffed at in the land
    that gave them birth!
"Scent of gum-leaves"—cease your jargon. 'Tis the
    finest scent on earth.
Ay, it clung around the Anzacs when they stormed
    Gallipoli;
And it steeps the nation-builders from the centre
    to the sea.
Speed the day when all united, heart to heart and
    hand to hand,
We'll proclaim the scent of gum-leaves to be
    sacred in the land.

    .   .   .   .   .

But my honeymooners leave me, and I watch them
    passing through—
They are homesick for the freshness of the open
    spaces, too—
So they gather up their bundles, and they wander
    home again
Back to where the morning magpies lather out the
    old refrain,
Back to love in fullest measure, pressed and flow-
    ing overtop,
Through the green months and the brown months,
    in the house behind the crop.
From the overcrowded city, from the bustle and
    the push
Pass my sturdy, happy couples who are sticking to
    the bush.

MAKING HOME

No, you don't quite get the meaning when the fun
    is at its height
With the neighbours at the breakfast, and the
    world is warm and bright;
And it doesn't come upon you when you're driv-
    ing to the train;
What with wrastling with the luggage, you've no
    time to feel the pain,
  But it grips you like a footpad, making home,
And you feel the sun will never drive the dark
    away again,
        Making home.

Yes, you go in with the rest to see your married
    girl away;
There's a mopy feeling round you, and you've
    nothing much to say;
So you crack a joke to mend things, but you make
    them worse instead.
Yet the loving words in hundreds are a-running
    through your head,

Welling from a heart that's melting, making
      home,
Interrupted by the stabbing of that wretched thing
      you said,
        Making home.

When the women start a-crying, just to show how
      glad they feel,
And you rouse upon "herself" a bit to keep the
      tears to heel,
It's a lot of silly business, and the whole thing gets
      you beat;
So before you realize it, you are climbing to the
      seat
  Of your buggy, with the missus, making home,
And the old horse clouts the metal with his heavy
      awkward feet,
        Making home.

You get glimpses through the timber of the lights
      a-sliding by,
You can see the red reflection palpitating in the
      sky;
You can hear the easy puffing as she swings into
      her stride,
And you feel a sort of pigmy in a world that's cold
      and wide,
  With the wise old stars above you, making
      home,
While you've got a notion someone is a-sobbing by
      your side,
        Making home.

Then the past shows up before you every ghost
    you thought had fled,
Everything you did unkindly, every peevish word
    you said;
And the poor old woman, battling with the tears
    that blind and ache,
She's been showering love around her all for
    someone else's sake,
  And it starts your mind a-wondering, making
    home,
Whether what you've been attending was a wed-
    ding or a wake,
        Making home.

So you pull up at the stable, take the harness off
    the horse,
Hit your shins against a bucket—well, it does no
    good, of course.
There's a gloom around the kitchen where the
    banquet still is spread,
And the cat upon the rocking-chair is sleeping
    like the dead,
  While the ghosts come leering at you, and you're
    home,
And "herself" she lights the candle, and she goes
    straight off to bed,
        When you're home.

But you don't feel much like sleeping with the
    throbbing in your brain,
And your heart is on a journey vagabonding with
    a train;
So you peel the choking collar off, and get out in
    the cool,
Where you light your pipe and smoke upon the old
    verandah stool,
    Thinking matters slowly over when you're
    home,
Winding back the skein that somehow's got
    entangled on the spool,
        When you're home.

Here's the little home you started when your hopes
    were all aglow;
Them's the currajongs you planted five-and-thirty
    year ago;
This here sixty-acre paddock was the first you
    called your own;
That there clearing was a forest, with the timber
    overgrown.
    So you start a-recollecting, when you're home.
Five-and-thirty years have flitted, and you don't
    know where they've flown,
        When you're home.

Here you've been along to-night to see the married
      girl away,
And you rocked her in her cradle—well, it seems
      but yesterday;
And "herself" you thought she looked so old, and
      bent and worn with care—
Five-and-thirty slaving winters pile the snows on
      heart and hair—
  And you find that you're an old man, making
      Home;
And the mile-posts on the road have got behind
      you unaware,
        Making Home.

There were joys your heart was craving, but you
      never gathered them;
Fragrant buds that yearned to blossom, but you
      hacked them from the stem;
Hearts of children, erring sometimes—ah, but
      golden through and through,
Beating back to where you led them, big with love
      of home and you!
  Now you see them in the distance, making
      Home,
Like the three red lights you watched to-night
      receding from your view,
        Making home.

So you sit with eyes wide open, seeing where
      you've been the fool,
Wise with wisdom born of sorrow, smoking,
      thinking in the cool,
Reckoning him God's new apostle who is busy
      being kind,
Hearing angel voices chant it in the music of the
      wind—
  Chastened, lonely, and so weary; making
      Home,
Praying God to pardon what you've been because
      your eyes were blind,
    Making Home.

COULD I HEAR THE KOOKABURRAS
ONCE AGAIN

May a fading fancy hover round a gladness that
   is over?
  May a dreamer in the silence rake the ashes of
    the past?
So a spirit might awaken in the best the years have
   taken,
  And the love that left him lonely might be with
    him at the last.
While he searches in the by-ways, shall his heart
   forget the highways
  Where the sunburnt arms are toiling in the sun-
    shine and the rain,
Where the simple things and lowly make their lives
   sublime and holy,
  And the kookaburras chorus once again?

There's a little house a-peeping o'er the swaying
   and the sweeping
  Of the wheat that nods and ripples as the breezes
    skim its top;
And the days of pioneering in the ringing and the
   clearing
  See the first-born of their labours in the house
    behind the crop.

There the fallow land is showing where the box
    and pine were growing,
  And a sweet hope gilds the future with the
    colour of the grain;
Gentle visions softly tripping in the ploughing and
    the stripping,
  While the kookaburras chorus once again.

Let a dying fancy hover round the glories that are
    over;
  Lift a song to sing the present—to the hopeless
    hope impart—
For above the past's bewailing, golden-writ but
    unavailing,
  Is the simple little ditty that can cheer a drooping
    heart.
Lift it high for all to hear it. In the Helper's love
    endear it,
  And my ageing heart shall hasten to applaud the
    sweet refrain;
Yes, I'd feel the pulses stirring to the splendid
    truth recurring,
  Could I hear the kookaburras once again.

Could I hear them as I heard them when the joy of
    living spurred them,
  When the world was clean and wholesome and
    they laughed the gloom away,
All the fatal fiction scorning that the canvas of the
    morning
  Is but splashed with faded colours from the
    brush of yesterday.

Oh, I'd bless them and I'd cheer them, could I
    wander off and hear them
  Boom the head-lights of the coming day that
    sweep the hills amain,
For I'd know the tocsin sounding of a fuller hope
    abounding,
  Could I hear them hail the dawning once
    again.

To no age in all the story of the bearded years and
    hoary
  Would I yield the future's promise in the mould
    of progress cast;
Still, a fading fancy lingers, while the touch of
    gentle fingers
  Moves aside the sombre curtain that was drawn
    across the past.
Come the fairy visions winging, come the laughter
    and the singing,
  But the shadows fall around me and the echo
    dies in pain;
Yet I'd feel the wings that bore me when the world
    was all before me,
  Could I hear the kookaburras once again.

COME, SING AUSTRALIAN SONGS
TO ME!

Come, Little One, and sing to me
    A song our big wide land to bless,
Around whose gentle parent-knee
    We've twined the flowers of kindliness.

Your eyes are clear Australian blue,
    Your voice like soft bush breezes blown;
Her sunshine steeps the heart of you,
    Your tresses are the wattle's own.

What, no Australian song, my child,
    No lay of love, no hymn of praise?
And yet no mother ever smiled
    With our dear country's winsome ways:

You sing the songs of all the earth,
    Of bower and bloom and bird and bee;
And has the land that gave you birth
    No haunting, native melody?

Your poets' eager pens awake
 The world-old themes of love and youth,
The pulse of life, the joy, the ache,
 The pregnant line of earnest truth;

They dress you these in native guise,
 And interweave with loving hand
The freshness of your rain-washed skies,
 The colours of your sunlit land.

What, no Australian song, my dear?
 And yet I've heard the cottage ring
With notes the world would pause to hear,
 When at their work your sisters sing.

They sing the songs of all the earth,
 Of tender sky, and dimpling sea,
But all their strains have not the worth
 Of one Australian song, for me.

I've heard the harp the breezes play
 Among the wilding wilga-trees;
I've swept my world of care away
 When bush birds lift their melodies;

I've seen the paddocks all ablaze
 When spring in golden glory comes,
The purple hills of summer days,
 The autumn ochres through the gums;

I've seen the bright folk riding in
   O'er blooms that deck the clovered plain,
And neath the trees, when moonbeams spin
   Their silver-dappled counterpane.

What, no Australian song, my pet?
   No patriot note on native horn,
To bind the hearts in kindness met,
   And link the leal Australian-born?

Yet every exile, wandering lone
   Our happy careless homes among,
May live the best his heart has known
   Whene'er his country's songs are sung.

You sing the songs of all the earth,
   Of alien flower and alien tree:
But no one, in my grief or mirth,
   Will sing Australian songs to me.

You sing of every land but mine,
   Where life is lilting neath the sun.
Still all its spirit seems ashine
   In you, my little laughing one.

Your eyes are clear Australian blue,
   Your face is towards the future set:
The bounding, gladsome heart of you
   Is hers—and only hers, my pet.

Ah, Little One, what dreams would rise
If, nestled here upon my knee,
You'd flash those soft Australian eyes,
And sing your country's songs to me!